# Tax Lien Investing Secrets

*How You Can Get 8% to 36% Return on Your Money Without the Typical Risk of Real Estate Investing or the Uncertainty of the Stock Market!*

*Joanne Musa*

# Tax Lien Investing Secrets
*How You Can Get 8% to 36% Return on Your Money Without the Typical Risk of Real Estate Investing or the Uncertainty of the Stock Market!*

ISBN-13: 978-1497426023
ISBN-10: 1497426022

© 2015 by Joanne Musa
This book is protected under the US Copyright Act of 1976 and all other applicable international, federal, state and local laws, with ALL rights reserved. No part of this may be copied, or changed in any format, sold, or used in any way other than is outlined within this book under any circumstances without express permission from Joanne M. Musa.

**Disclaimer:** The author and publisher of this book and accompanying materials have used their best efforts in preparing this book. The author and publisher make no representation or warranties with respect to the accuracy, applicability, fitness, or completeness of the contents of this book. The information in this book is strictly for educational purposes. Therefore, if you wish to apply ideas contained in this book, you are taking full responsibility for your actions.

The author and publisher disclaim any warranties, (express or implied), merchantability, or fitness for any particular purpose. Neither the author nor the publisher shall be held liable to any party for any direct, indirect, punitive, special, incidental or other consequential damages arising directly or indirectly from any use of this material, which is provided "as is," and without warranties. The author is not engaged in providing legal, accounting or financial advice. If professional assistance is required, the advice of a competent legal, tax, accounting or other professional should be sought. The author and publisher do not warrant the performance, effectiveness or applicability of any websites listed or linked to in this book, since they may have changed or been removed in the time from when this book was written and when it is read. All links are for information purposes only and are not warranted for content, accuracy or any other implied or explicit purpose.

Brand names are © copyrighted by their respective companies. No claims or endorsements are implied by their use or recommendation.

You should assume that the author and publisher may have an affiliate relationship and/or another material connection to the providers of goods and services mentioned in this book and may be compensated when you purchase from a provider. You should always perform due diligence before buying goods or services from anyone via the Internet or offline.

**Her Guidance Is Top Notch**

"If you are looking for a solution to Tax Lien and Deed investing you've come to the right place with The Tax Lien Lady. I started my search years ago with other providers without a single result, until I found Joanne Musa. Her coaching program has delivered, and her guidance is top notch."

Steve Iltz (Investor, Oregon)

**Integrity and vast, nationwide knowledge**

"Joanne's presence in the industry is steady and true, and she fully believes in providing quality, education opportunities for individual investors. At TSR, we always feel confident sending novice investors or those looking to expand into new jurisdictions to Joanne. We know that she will take good care of any investor and provide them the important education necessary in making wise, "no-hype" decisions before investing their hard-earned money. Joanne stands above others in her class with her integrity and vast, nationwide knowledge that many others cannot provide."

Rachel A. Seidensticker (COO, TaxSaleResources.com)

**Great Information From A High Level**

"As a professional investor since 2001, I'm always looking to learn more and get an edge on other real estate investors. The problem is typically finding a trusted source. Thankfully, Joanne Musa has generously written a book that gives great information from a high level, but then gets granular regarding selecting the best places to invest, breaking down bidding and of course due diligence so you don't get burned. The great news is you can google 'The Tax Lien Lady Joanne Musa' and she is not just a teacher, but also a professional investor herself. This is the type of mentor I look for when getting information on investing, especially in a niche like tax liens. If you are remotely interested in tax lien investing and learning how to get high returns with minimal risk then I would wholeheartedly recommend this book to be a helpful addition to your investing book collection."

Mark Podolsky (Founder, TheLandGeek.com)

**Great Info – No Hype**

"It's refreshing to read a book on tax liens that doesn't hype the investment and promise 'pennies on the dollar' riches like other books -- she knowledgeably and thoroughly covers the subject of this niche market in a way that was easy to read. If you're looking for a 'why' to get into buying tax liens -- ready this book first. By the way, there really are no 'secrets' to tax liens but the information is so scattered and hard-to-find, it's great when you have one resource to go to vs doing all the research yourself!"

Jeff Frantz (CEO, TaxDeed360.com)

# Table of Contents

Table of Contents ................................................................... vii
   Acknowledgements ............................................................. ix
   Foreword ........................................................................... xi
   Introduction ..................................................................... xiii
PART I Getting Started ........................................................ 23
   CHAPTER ONE: The Basics of Tax Lien Investing ..................... 25
   CHAPTER TWO: 5 Steps to Buying Profitable Tax Liens ........... 29
   CHAPTER THREE: Selecting the Best Place to Invest ................ 33
   CHAPTER FOUR: Tracking Down the Tax Sale Information ...... 41
   CHAPTER FIVE: Evaluating Tax Sale Properties ........................ 47
   CHAPTER SIX: Preparing To Go To the Sale ............................ 55
   CHAPTER SEVEN: Bidding At The Tax Sale ............................. 59
PART II Managing Your Portfolio ........................................ 67
   CHAPTER EIGHT: Protecting Your Profit .................................. 69
   CHAPTER NINE: Cashing In On Your Investment ..................... 77
   CHAPTER TEN: Automating Your Investing ............................. 83
PART III More Ways to Invest ............................................ 87
   CHAPTER ELEVEN: Done For You Investing ............................ 89
   CHAPTER TWELVE: Investing From Afar ................................. 95
   CHAPTER THIRTEEN: Secondary Tax Liens ............................ 103
   CHAPTER FOURTEEN: Investing For Your Future ................. 105

CHAPTER FIFTEEN: More Tips for Your Success ...................... 109
Conclusion & Resources ................................................................ 113
Epilogue ......................................................................................... 115
Glossary.......................................................................................... 121
About The Author .......................................................................... 129

# Acknowledgements

I am indebted to the subscribers to my blog and various websites, to my students who have taken my tax lien investing courses over the years, to my members who join me for monthly trainings and to my coaching clients. Your feedback, encouragement and success is what makes me want to continue to teach what I know, and keep learning more about the tax lien investing market. I especially like hearing your success stories.

I would also like to thank everyone who has helped me, both in the field of tax lien investing and in learning all the technical stuff that I needed to be able to do in order to take my knowledge and share it online. One person that I learned from early on and has been instrumental in my online success as well as creating all of my courses, e-books, and this book, is Jeanette Cates. I have taken many of her courses and I have been a student of Jeanette's since I have been online (over 10 years). Thank you Jeanette for all of your help and inspiration!

I'd like to thank all of the tax lien investing and tax deed experts that I've interviewed over the years including Steve Waters, Darius Barazandeh, Rick Dawson, and Jack Bosch, and more recently Mark Podolsky, Ryan Roberts, Tom DiAgostino, and Corey Taylor.

And those I've interviewed and learned from who provide services for the tax lien industry, Steve Davis of LienSource, Brian Seidensticker and Rachel Seidensticker of Tax Sale Resources, Philipe Soares, Dave Schumacher, and Bob Shakman of Tax Title Services and tax lien investing attorney and author Mike Pellegrino.

The agents and fund managers that I have learned from over the years including Charles Sells and Don Fullman of Platinum Investment Properties Group, Arnie Abramson of Texas Tax Sale Resource Group, Kate Dougherty Jones of Comian Investment Group, Ashley

Anisfeld of Stonefield Investments, and David Farber of Pro Capital LLC.

The IRA custodians that have done informative webinars with me for my subscribers and customers, and who I continue to learn from, especially Carl Fischer of CAMA Plan and Belinda Savage of IRA Services. And a thank you to Equity Trust Company for inviting me to be on their tax lien investing panel at their networking event for three years in a row.

And I can't forget the man who helped me get started in this business when he hired me to invest for him in New Jersey back in 2002, John Proske of DataVentures, LLC.

This book would not have been possible without the help of my assistants Debby, and Karen, and a special thank you to my family, especially my husband Bill who put up with me while I spent untold hours writing this book.

# Foreword

Now that you acquired and opened this book, do yourself a huge favor and be certain to finish it in the next 36-48hrs. Then immediately using Joanne's easy to follow steps; determine where you want to invest, get the tax sale information, quickly evaluate the tax sale properties, prepare the bid, and lastly capture your winning tax sale bid or bids. If my four foot eleven inch friend can do it, you better believe you can.

Joanne and I have both a personal and professional relationship, which spans quite a few years. As a much disciplined, wildly successful weightlifter now competing at the Masters level, she eloquently and gracefully with acute aplomb deploys the same skill as the accomplished Tax Lien Lady.

My background is in residential real estate valuation. Having been an Appraiser licensed simultaneously in three southeastern states and founder of InvestorCompsOnline to serve investors both domestically and internationally, it is with honor I acknowledge Joanne's numerous achievements. Especially the care and fortitude in discovering tax lien investing for herself. Subsequently selflessly sharing the power of this truly dynamic investing model with those who desire to avoid risk and earn easily attainable double-digit returns.

Our friendship began as a result of Joanne's commitment to provide a core component to her clients which was sorely needed. The ability to valuate tax sale properties. and her diligent search brought us together. Joanne frankly has always tenaciously searched to provide the absolute best tools and resources for her clients. This exact same care for her clients is present throughout her teaching and training of tax lien investing, which is now in your very possession.

In this book you will seamlessly discover details of tax lien investing moving you forward quickly and easily. Joanne shares details other so called experts would prefer to keep a secret. One quality you will note rather swiftly is the simple way she makes complex concepts easy to digest and consume. As such, your ability to take swift action will make your tax lien business boundless in its potential success.

One of the absolute delights of this book is Joanne's relentless listing of resources that automate your business. Her Tax Lien Management software will literally put your business on autopilot. However, if you prefer a hands-on approach, know each item handled by the software is first explained in bite size pieces so you may capture every detail. This is the beauty of Joanne and her care for you as a new or seasoned tax lien investor.

Truly, Joanne's years in the arena of tax lien investing, first successfully investing herself, are to be herald. Then taking her well-honed skills to people like you across the US and abroad has proven invaluable. I consider her a trusted colleague and friend whose actions and character are solidly grounded in a principled respect for the needs and aspirations of investors, especially those who desire something not just for themselves, but for their loved ones. Her legacy as a mother, wife, accomplished athlete, weightlifting coach, business person, and naturally, tax lien investor lay the foundation for generations of others to follow.

I am not only proud she has committed to written work her teachings here, I am grateful to call her my very dear friend.

Mark Jackson, B.S., CREA
Founder of InvestorCompsOnline.com
Author, Appraiser Secrets for Real Estate Investors
Atlanta, GA and Denver, CO

# Introduction

## Preparing For Economic Disaster

Are you concerned about what's happening with the economy and would you like to know how to prepare for what's ahead? The top financial and economic experts in North America do not have good things to say about the state of the U.S. economy, and about where the economies of the most prominent nations of the world are headed for the next few years. You don't have to read their financial newsletters to figure out that governments and the media are not telling the whole story about the job market, the real estate market, the stock market and the U.S. dollar. All you have to do is look around.

How many people do you know that are out of work right now and have been out of work for a while? Or how many young people do you know that have just finished their secondary education and are having a heck of a time finding a job in their field? I don't know how things are where you live, but there are a few vacant houses in my neighborhood. These are houses that have been taken back by the bank. How many houses are there in your neighborhood that have been for sale for over a year? I know right down the street from me there is a house that has been for sale for at least 2 years. This house was taken over by the bank when the previous owners couldn't sell it, and now the bank is not able to sell it either. Gas and heating oil prices are outrageous, food is getting more expensive, and it's tougher to get a loan or to refinance an existing loan. These are the signs of the times.

One of my subscribers (a young man from Hawaii) describes the state of the U.S. economy like this:

"...the emperor has no clothes. There is no money in the treasury...nothing but mothballs and cobwebs...we have a legacy of debt hidden by a good name...but the rest of the countries of the world are coming to that realization, which is why they are abandoning the dollar as the reserve currency and why the U.S. credit rating has already been downgraded and will likely soon be downgraded again...

The emperor has no clothes...I am sure that you have heard this in the wind lately..."

He actually wrote this to me two years ago, but not much has changed since.

He's right, the emperor has no cloths! Baby boomers are concerned about their retirement and their investments. Are you concerned about the safety of your retirement account? How would you like to invest your money without worrying about another stock market crash, in an investment where your money will keep getting the same high return regardless of what happens to the market. What if your return is mandated by state law and is guaranteed by real property, not a just a piece of paper... would that be of interest to you?

## Introduction | xv

For over 10 years now I've been showing my subscribers how to prepare for what's ahead, protect their retirement, and profit from high yielding, real estate guaranteed, U.S. tax lien certificates. In my webinars and online home study courses, I teach my 5 STEPS method to purchasing profitable tax liens, and how to protect your investment in tax lien certificates and tax deeds after you purchase them, as well as how to profit from them.

Don't listen to the hype, tax lien investing is NOT a way to get property for pennies on the dollar - almost all good tax lien certificates redeem. IT IS the best way I know of to invest your money safely and grow your wealth virtually risk free. The wealthy have been profiting from tax lien certificates for years and now you can do it too.

Right now there are hundreds of tax sales scheduled to take place, and some of these tax sales are online. If you are looking to secure your retirement, and you'd like to learn more about tax liens and tax deeds visit my blog at TaxLienInvestingTips.com

### A Safer Alternative to Investing In the Stock Market

The stock market recently took another tumble at the time of the writing of the first draft of this book, but it didn't concern me at all. I have very little invested in the market. Most of my money is invested in tax lien certificates and the interest I make on my tax liens does not fluctuate with the market. In fact that interest rate is guaranteed by the county or municipal government that issues the lien.

There is a better way to invest your money - you can get double digit returns without putting your money at the risk of the markets. Tax lien investing is a great alternative to investing in stocks and now is as good a time as any to invest in tax liens. Let's start out with some basic information about tax lien investing. What is a tax lien anyway?

## What Is a Tax Lien Certificate?

Counties and municipalities depend on money from property taxes to meet their budget. When property owners don't pay their taxes, the county or municipality will sell the taxes to an investor. The investor is not buying the property but paying the taxes on the property and putting a lien on the property.

## Why Would You Want to Pay Someone Else's Taxes?

There are three very good reasons to buy a tax lien certificate and pay someone else's taxes. First, in many states, tax lien certificates earn high interest rates dictated by state laws. These rates can be much higher than what your money would make on other safe investments, and certainly better than you could do in a bank CD or money market account. Secondly, a tax lien comes before most other liens, so the tax lien investor is first in line to get paid, even before a mortgage or loan on the property. Third, if the property owner doesn't pay off the lien in a certain period of time, the tax lien holder can foreclose on the property. Now that's incentive for the property owner to pay off the lien!

## What is the difference between tax lien and tax deed investing?

In some states, when a property owner does not pay their taxes, instead of selling a lien on the property, the county or municipality will sell the property at a tax deed sale. In states that sell tax deeds, you are actually buying the property. In some states, the property is sold for back taxes and penalties, in other states the property is sold for a certain percentage of its assessed value, and in a couple of deed states, the property is sold at market value. A tax deed can be a good investment, especially in states that sell the property for the back taxes because the investor has a chance to buy real estate at a price that is considerably under market value.

## What is a Redeemable Tax Deed?

Some states sell what is referred to as "redeemable" tax deeds. The deed to the property is sold (auctioned) at the tax sale, but there is a redemption period in which the delinquent taxpayer can come back and redeem the property. In order to redeem the property the delinquent taxpayer must pay the investor the bid price plus a hefty penalty or interest on the bid price. Some redeemable deed states have a penalty and some have an interest rate. In some states, the penalty or interest can be quite high, making it very attractive to the investor.

## What are some of the misconceptions about this type of investment?

Because people have been told that tax liens are a great investment and that they can make such high interest, they assume that interest is paid out by the county or municipality on a regular basis. The truth about tax lien investing is that you do not get paid a cent until the delinquent property owner decides to redeem the lien. If the property owner does not redeem the lien during the redemption period (which is different for every state) then the investor can foreclose on the property.

Another misunderstanding about tax lien investing is that after the redemption period is over, the lien holder will automatically get the deed to the property. The truth about foreclosing on a tax lien is that in most states you need a lawyer in order to foreclose and get the deed to the property. There are some states where you don't have to go through a judicial process and you can simply apply for a deed. In Florida the property will be sold in a tax deed sale, and will be auctioned to the highest bidder in order to satisfy the lien.

Some people have the misunderstanding that tax lien investing is a good way to buy properties for pennies on the dollar. The truth is that a tax lien on a good property will almost always redeem. Even when an investor has the opportunity to foreclose the right of redemption, the tax lien can redeem at any time during the foreclosure process. Tax lien investing is a way to get a high return on your money, not a good way to get property. If you are interested in buying property for under market value, you are better off with tax deeds or redeemable tax deeds. We will talk more about the difference between tax liens, tax deeds and redeemable tax deed in Chapter 1.

**Is Tax Lien Investing For You?**

Tax lien investing used to be something that only the wealthy knew about and took advantage of. For decades, it was a little known, high yielding investment vehicle. All of this has changed in the past few years as more and more people become aware of the high yields and minimal risk of investing in tax lien certificates. Many people have heard about investing in tax lien certificates but they are not sure if it's really something that they can do.

Tax lien certificates are an attractive investment for the small investor because you don't need to have thousands of dollars to start investing, and you don't have to pay any brokerage fees. There are drawbacks, however. You almost have to become an expert in tax lien investing to invest profitably. This is an investment that you have to be able to devote some time to. It's not like you can call your broker and tell him to buy some tax liens for your portfolio. Tax lien certificates are sold at tax sales conducted by a county or municipal official. These sales are usually auctions that are held at least once a year.

You have to find out when and where these tax sales are, get the tax sale information and rules, do your due diligence on the properties in the sale, and decide which properties to bid on and how much to bid. Then you have to attend the tax sale to bid on properties (or bid online in some instances). When you are the successful bidder, you are issued a tax lien certificate or tax deed and in some states you are responsible to record the certificate or deed with the county clerk. Some states will hold on to the certificate and simply send you a receipt and you do not have to record your lien in these states. After purchasing a tax lien, you are then responsible for maintaining accurate records and submitting the proper documents to safeguard your investment.

If you have the time to spend researching properties and you enjoy the challenge of learning something new, then perhaps investing in tax lien certificates could be a good way for you to increase your bottom line. If, however, you don't have the time to spend researching properties and finding out about tax sales, there are ways that you can have experts invest for you (and do all the other work). You'll find more detail about that in Chapter 11.

Another thing to consider is your location. Some states do not sell tax liens, and if you do not live in a state that has tax lien sales, you may have to spend a considerable amount of money traveling to tax sales in order to buy tax lien certificates. Although some counties have online auctions or sell tax liens through the mail, you would still have to do due diligence on properties before you place a bid. If you do not do your due diligence, you could lose money by buying a tax lien certificate or tax deed on a worthless piece of property.

**Why You Might Want to Invest In Tax Liens**

I consider tax liens to be a superior investment for the following seven reasons:

1. Where else can you get 8 - 36% on your money without the risk of the stock market?

2. Your investment is secured by real estate, which will have a value many times your original investment (if you do your homework). Even if the real estate market takes a tumble, the property securing your money should still be worth more than you invested.

3. Since you do not have to go through someone else to purchase a tax lien, there are no brokerage fees.

4. Unlike other real estate investments, you don't need a lot of money to start. You can start investing with a small amount of money.

5. You don't need good credit, you don't have to open a special account, and you don't even need to be a U.S. citizen or live in the U.S. to invest in tax liens or tax deeds.

6. You can invest in some areas from home using your computer.

7. You can invest with funds from your Self-directed IRA.

There are more reasons why I consider investing in tax lien certificates to be a superior way to invest my money safely but these are the 7 main reasons why I like tax lien investing.

## What Tax Lien Investing Isn't

Beware of those that make it sound too easy, if it were that easy everyone would already be doing it. Tax lien investing is a great way to grow your wealth, but it's not a way to get rich quick. Beware of gurus that tell you that you can make a lot of money by only investing a couple of hundred dollars in tax liens. Even if you make 36% on your money, unless you have a considerable amount to invest you are not going to make a living off your profit. Investing in tax lien certificates is not a way to get the property, most tax liens redeem, and very, very seldom will you get the chance to foreclose on a property. Even if you did get to foreclose on a property, you would have to pay the taxes on the property while you waited out the redemption period, which can be as long as 3 years in some states.

Although some tax lien investing "experts" make it sound like you're guaranteed to get paid on a tax lien, this is simply not true. The only thing guaranteeing payment on your lien is the property. That's why it's so important to do your due diligence before buying a tax lien. You also have to make sure that you understand the terms and conditions of the tax sale and the bidding procedures. Each state handles these tax sales differently and you have to make sure that you know the rules of the game before you play! You'll find out more about what you need to know about due diligence and bidding in Chapters 3 and 5.

Buying profitable tax liens is really quite simple. Anyone can learn how to buy profitable tax lien certificates with the right guidance. You only really need to do 2 things. The first is to buy liens on good properties and the second is to be able to get the money out of your lien. We'll cover what you need to know to buy good liens in Part 1 (chapters 1-7). Then we'll cover what you need to do after you purchase a tax lien in order to protect your investment in chapter 8.

There are 3 ways that you can cash out of your lien. Either the lien will redeem, or if the lien does not redeem you can foreclose on the property. If you don't want to wait for redemption or for the opportunity to foreclose, you can sell your lien to another investor. You'll discover how you cash out on your investment and ways to profit faster from your liens in Chapter 9. In Chapter 10 you'll learn how to automate and streamline your investing. And in the remaining chapters I'll clue you in about different ways to invest in tax liens that you probably have never thought of: Ways that you can have experts do it for you (chapter 11), ways to invest from a distance (chapter 12), ways to invest in tax liens that are ready to foreclose now (chapter 13), ways to invest with your self-directed IRA (chapter 14), and how to get more tips about tax lien investing (chapter 15).

My hope is that this book will enlighten you with the truth about tax lien investing, not just the hype and fluff that is given out in a lot of real estate investing and "wealth building" seminars. I want to give you enough information, encouragement and motivation, and enough ways to invest that you will find one that resonates with you. I want you to be able to stop learning about it and start doing it correctly and profitably, so that you make a difference in your financial future.

One more thing before you read the rest of this book. Anyone who tells you they are an expert on tax lien investing everywhere in the country is not being truthful. Tax lien investing and redeemable deed investing is so different in every state, that one person could not be an expert in every state. Frankly, some states are just not worth investing in. Therefore, while you will find some information on some states in this book, you won't find detailed how to information on every state in any book you pick up about tax lien investing, unless it's an encyclopedia! I have found that books and guides that claim to do this are just a compilation of the laws in each state. They tell you what the law allows in each state, but not what actually happens. Sometimes what the law allows and what actually happens are 2 different things and you want to know what procedures you actually have to follow. If you want specific information on how to invest in a certain state, contact me at info@taxlienlady.com and I can recommend the best resource for your particular situation, because one size does not fit all when it comes to tax lien investing knowledge.

# PART I Getting Started

# CHAPTER ONE: The Basics of Tax Lien Investing

## What is the Difference between a Tax Lien and a Tax Deed?

So many new tax lien investors don't know the difference between a tax lien and tax deed. They've heard that tax liens are a great investment and that you can get the property with a tax lien. They confuse tax liens and tax deeds. For those of you who think that buying a tax lien is a good way to get property, that is not really the truth.

As I mentioned in the Introduction, tax lien investing is not a good way to get property for back taxes. When you purchase a tax lien, you are not purchasing the property. You are simply paying the property owner's taxes and getting the interest and the penalties that the government would normally collect. One of the reasons that tax liens are such a good investment is that if the lien is not redeemed within a given amount of time, then the lien holder can foreclose on the property.

It is very seldom that a tax lien on a good property will not redeem. The investor hardly ever gets to foreclose on the property. Unless you specialize in buying liens on vacant land, or on properties that have a particular problem that you might be able to solve, or if do not do your homework and you buy liens on junk properties, you are not likely to get the property. Tax lien investing, while it is a great way to invest your money at a high return, is not a way to buy properties for a fraction of their value. However, investing in tax deeds or redeemable tax deeds can be.

## Tax Deeds

What is different about a tax deed is that when you purchase a tax deed you are actually purchasing the property, not just the taxes. When you get a deed at a tax deed sale, or if you purchase a tax deed directly from the county, you are actually purchasing the property. The deed issued is usually a non-warrantee deed. In most deed states (there are a couple of exceptions) the property is conveyed free of any liens, but there is no warrantee on the title. You may have to clear the title before you can get title insurance for the property. As the tax deed purchaser, you also may have to evict the current inhabitants of the property, but you are the legal owner of the property as soon as the deed is recorded.

## Redeemable Tax Deeds

A redeemable tax deed is something in between a tax lien and tax deed. I have heard it referred to by some investors as a "tax lien deed." When you go to a redeemable tax deed sale, you are actually purchasing the deed to the property. If you are the successful bidder, you will receive a tax deed to the property. The deed however, is encumbered for a given amount of time, known as the redemption period (similar to the redemption period for tax liens). The owner can redeem the property by paying the bid amount, plus a hefty penalty. If the deed is not redeemed during the redemption period, than the previous owner is barred from redeeming the property and the tax deed holder is the owner of record and the legal owner of the property. This process is very different in each redeemable deed state. In some states, it is automatic and in others you have to actually hire an attorney and foreclose the right to redeem the deed, just as you do with a tax lien.

## Which is Better, Redeemable Deeds or Tax Liens?

A redeemable tax deed is very similar to tax lien, but there are some important differences that I believe make redeemable tax deeds a better deal for the investor. I will point out that every redeemable deed state treats these deeds differently. In Texas for example, when you purchase a redeemable deed you are the legal owner of the property and can evict anyone who may be in the property once the deed is recorded. If there is a tenant in the property, you can collect the rent. The previous owner has redemption rights, but is no longer the rightful owner of the property.

In Georgia, which is another popular redeemable deed state, when you purchase a deed you are not the legal owner of the property until the redemption period is over and you foreclose on the property. In Georgia, you must foreclose the right to redeem the deed (just as you would in most tax lien states) in order to take ownership of the property.

In both Georgia and Texas (and other redeemable deed states) in order to redeem the deed, the property owner must pay the investor what they bid at the tax sale plus a hefty penalty – not an annualized interest rate. This means is that if you purchase a redeemable tax deed and it redeems a few days after you record the deed you still get the full penalty amount. You make the same return on your money if it redeems in 2 weeks as you do if it redeems in 6 months. A penalty is not annualized, like an interest payment is.

**What are the Drawbacks to Investing in Redeemable Deeds as Opposed to Tax Liens?**

There are only 7 states that sell redeemable tax deeds and none of these states have online tax sales, so you have to show up for the auction in order to participate in the sale. The 7 states that do sell redeemable tax deeds are Connecticut, Delaware, Georgia, Hawaii, South Carolina, Tennessee, and Texas. In Connecticut tax sales are conducted by the municipality, not the county, and each municipality can decide whether it wants to sell redeemable deeds or tax liens. So not all towns in Connecticut sell redeemable deeds, some of the larger cities will have tax lien sales instead.

# CHAPTER TWO: 5 Steps to Buying Profitable Tax Liens

There are some simple steps that you need to take in order to buy profitable tax liens or tax deeds. Here is what I call my 5 STEPS System to purchasing profitable tax liens. I use the word STEPS as an acronym to help you remember what they are.

**S**elect the right place to invest
**T**rack down the tax sale information
**E**valuate the tax sale properties
**P**repare to attend the sale
**S**how up and bid

## STEP 1: Select the Right Place to Invest

So many people ask me, "where is the best place to invest in tax liens," and, "which are the best states to invest in?" However, the truth is that the best place for me to invest might not be the best place for you to invest. The best state for you to invest in depends on your answers to these questions:

- Are you interested in investing your money for high returns or do you want to own and manage property?
- What state do you live in?
- Where do you like to vacation?
- How much money do you have to invest?
- Are you investing with money from your retirement account or after tax money?
- Are you looking for a short term or long-term investment?

If you don't have much money to invest than you really need to get started with tax liens and not tax deeds or redeemable deeds. If you would like to get the property and not just a high return on your money, than you are better off investing in deed states or redeemable deed states. It is not very wise to invest in a state just because it's the most profitable place to invest, especially if you have to travel a few thousand miles to attend a tax sale. The first thing that you need to do is to find the state closest to you where it would make sense for you to invest based on your answers to the previous questions. In the next chapter, I'll go over the six things you need to know before selecting where to invest. For now, let's go on to the second step in our 5 STEPS System.

## STEP 2: Track Down the Tax Sale Information

Once you've selected the right place to invest, you need to get the tax sale information: The bidding procedures for the tax sale, the location and time of the tax sale, the terms of the sale, and the tax sale list. There are resources and tools available to help you with this, but you can usually get the information that you need by calling the party responsible for the tax sale. Usually that will be the county treasurer or county tax collector. If you can't find the information that way, then there are tax sale list providers that will provide this information for a fee. Buying the enhanced tax sale lists from a list provider will cut down the time it takes for you to evaluate and choose which properties to bid on (STEP 3). I'll cover how to get the tax sale information a little more in depth in chapter 4.

## STEP 3: Evaluate the Tax Sale Properties

This is probably the most important step in the process. It involves doing your due diligence on the properties in the tax sale to see which ones are worth bidding on. When evaluating the properties you need to have a way to track the information for each property. You need to know more about the properties in a tax deed sale than you will for tax lien properties. Even for tax liens, you want to know that the property is valuable before you purchase a lien on it.

For both liens and deeds, you want to know the tax assessment data of the properties in the tax sale and see what the property looks like from the street. It is also nice to know when a property was last sold, what the sale price was, and whether or not there is a mortgage on the property. You want to make sure that there are no environmental problems on or near the property. This information can be found online for most states, but sometimes you will have to go to the county assessment office or county hall of records to get the information that you need. For tax deed properties, you also need to know if there are any other liens, judgments, or encumbrances on the properties, and whether proper notifications of the tax sale were made to all parties with an interest in the property.

Doing this step properly can make or break your investment and this is not meant to be a systematic guide to take you through this process. We will go a little more into how to do due diligence on tax sale properties in chapter 5. I also have home study courses and coaching programs that cover all of these steps more thoroughly if you feel you need more help. My Build Your Profitable Tax Lien Portfolio (at ProfitableTaxLienPortfolio.com) course has a whole lesson on how to do due diligence for tax liens and tax deeds, and my Online Tax Deed Sales course (at OnlineTaxDeeds.com) covers how to do due diligence for tax deed properties online. There are also multiple trainings on this in the Tax Lien Profits Accelerator™ (Tax Lien Lady's Members Area).

**STEP 4: Prepare to Bid at the Tax Sale**

Now that you have the tax sale information and you have done your due diligence and determined which properties you will bid on, it is time to get ready to go to the tax sale. You have to register to bid and make sure that you have the proper form of payment for any successful bids that you might have. Make sure that you understand the terms of the sale and bidding procedures and that you complete any necessary paperwork. You will need a tax ID number in order to bid at tax liens sale and you will need to supply a W-9 form. (Foreigners will need to have a W-8BEN form). See chapter 6 for more help with this step and chapter 12 for tips on investing from outside the U.S.

**STEP 5: Show Up And Bid At The Tax Sale!**

Now it's time to show up and bid at the tax sale. If the tax sale is live and not online, make sure that you get there early, with plenty of time to get any updates of liens or deeds that have been removed from the list, and to get a good seat. Make sure that you don't have any distractions. Tax sales are auctions and things happen very fast. It helps to have a bid sheet with you listing all of the properties in the tax sale (in the order they will be auctioned) with those that you want to bid on marked with the amount you are prepared to bid. Do not get carried away and bid more than your pre-determined amount for a property and do not bid on any properties that you did not investigate first! Pay for any successful bids on time or they may be re-bid and you'll find yourself barred from future tax sales.

In the next chapters, we go a little more in depth on how to accomplish these 5 STEPS. In order to help you select the right place to invest, the next chapter explores the 6 things you need to know before you bid.

# CHAPTER THREE: Selecting the Best Place to Invest

*If you believe the hype that you hear about tax lien investing, you would think that you just go to a tax sale, buy some liens and make loads of money in a few months. If that were true than everybody would be doing it!*

If you have actually started to invest in tax liens then you know that there is some work involved in order to be successful. You know that you have to do your due diligence on tax sales properties. You also know that those double-digit interest rates that everyone talks about are bid down at the tax sale.

## The Six Things You Need To Know

There are **6 things that you need to know** about tax lien or tax deed investing before you get started.

1. **The statutory interest rate** – this is the rate that the county charges delinquent tax payers and the rate that investors get on their money when it is not bid down at the tax sale.
2. **The bidding method** – What is actually bid at the tax sale, whether the amount paid for the lien is bid up, or the interest rate is bid down, or something else entirely is bid, or there is no bidding at all and winners are randomly chosen.
3. **The redemption period** – The period of time that the property owner has to redeem the lien or redeemable deed before the lien holder can foreclose on the property.
4. **The expiration period** – The "life" of the tax lien, after which the lien will expire worthless if no action is taken by the investor.

5. **How subsequent taxes are handled** – Whether or not the lien holder gets to pay the subsequent taxes if the property owner doesn't pay them, and what interest or penalties are paid on the subsequent tax payments.
6. **Additional Penalties** – Are there other penalties that the lien holder gets when the lien or redeemable deed redeems?

These six things make a huge difference in your profit and are the reason why tax lien investing is very different in different states. Let me give you examples from three different states that all have auctions where the interest rate is bid down, but because of the other 5 factors mentioned in this chapter, investing in each of these states is quite different.

**New Jersey**

In New Jersey, the statutory interest rate is 18% and the interest rate is bid down at the tax sale. However, it is quite a different process from other states in which the interest rate is bid down because in NJ the interest rate can be bid down to 0% and then premium is bid for liens. Premium is an amount over and above the amount of the tax lien that investors are willing to pay in order get the lien. Each state in which premium is bid handles it differently, In New Jersey, you do not get any interest on the certificate amount (since it has already been bid down to 0%) and you do not get any interest on the premium. The premium is returned to the investor (without interest) if the lien redeems within 5 years. The redemption period is 2 years and the lien expires in 20 years.

Why would investors pay premium for liens and not get any interest on the lien amount? Investors are willing to pay premium for tax liens in New Jersey because once you are the lien holder, you have the right to pay the subsequent taxes on the property (if the owner fails to pay them on time) and you get the statutory interest rate (18%) on your subsequent tax payments. You also receive a penalty amount of 2-6%

on the certificate amount (depending on the dollar amount of the lien) when the tax lien is redeemed. I have simplified the process a little, but that is basically how it works in NJ. Large premiums are paid at New Jersey tax sales because of the added penalty amounts and the interest paid on subsequent tax payments.

**Florida**

Florida is similar to New Jersey in that the statutory interest rate is 18%, the interest rate is bid down at the tax sale, and the redemption period is two years. That is where the similarities between the processes in these two states end. The bidding in Florida is a little different than in NJ. In Florida, you do not get to pay the subsequent taxes on your lien until the redemption period is over. If the owner doesn't pay the taxes, the property will wind up in next year's tax sale. The interest rate is bid down at the tax sale, and the lien expires in 7 years. Bidders will frequently bid down the interest rate to .25%. They do this because they will get a 5% minimum penalty when the lien redeems. If the lien does not redeem, you do not get to foreclose on the lien as you do in other states. Instead, you apply for the lien to go to a tax deed sale in order to satisfy your lien. At this point, you need to pay all the subsequent taxes and redeem any subsequent liens, but you will get the statutory rate (18%) on all of your subsequent tax payments if the lien redeems sometime after you make the deed application or is sold in the deed sale.

**Arizona**

In Arizona, the statutory interest rate is 16%, and the interest rate is bid down as it is in Florida and New Jersey. However, the interest is rarely bid down as low as in the other two states. The redemption period is three years and the lien expires in 10 years. You can pay the subsequent taxes but you only get the interest rate that you bid at the tax sale on your subsequent tax payments. Some counties in Arizona actually force you to pay the subsequent taxes if you want to hold on to your lien. In these counties, if the subsequent taxes go unpaid, they will sell the prior lien with the current lien in the next tax sale. Interest rates in Arizona counties of late are bid down to lower than 5 or 6% (at least in the online tax sales), 7-9% have been the average for vacant land. Investors rarely bid down as low in Arizona as they do in Florida and New Jersey for three reasons. First, there are no added penalties in Arizona. Second, you only get the interest that is bid at the tax sale on the subsequent tax payments. Third, Arizona counties have extra handling charges per lien which are added into the lien and do not bear interest, effectively lowering your return, especially on smaller liens.

Even among these three states, which have similar interest rates, bidding procedures, and redemption periods, there is quite a difference in how they treat subsequent tax payments, and penalties. There are also states that have very different bidding procedures, redemption periods, expiration periods, and treatment of subsequent tax payments, which can change the game quite a bit. Maryland is one example:

**Maryland**

In Maryland, the statutory interest rate varies with the county. Premium is bid at the tax sale but the entire premium amount does not have to be paid unless you actually get to foreclose on the property. The redemption period in some counties is only 6 months, and the lien expires in 2 years. You do not pay the subsequent taxes unless you foreclose on the property. There are no additional penalties except for payment of some legal costs if the investor has already begun the foreclosure process.

Now that you understand how important it is to know about these 6 factors in the state and county that you are investing in, let's look at each of these things a little more in depth.

## Statutory Interest Rate

The statutory interest rate is the interest rate that the county will charge the delinquent taxpayer. It is also the interest that the investor will receive on the amount of the lien if it is not bid down at the tax sale. Just because a state has a statutory interest rate of 18% does not mean that if you go to a tax sale and purchase a tax lien you will get an 18% return on your investment. That depends on the next thing you need to know, which is the bidding method.

## Bidding Method

Each state has a different process for bidding. In some states, the interest rate is bid down, as described in Arizona, Florida, and New Jersey. In these states, the investor who is willing to accept the lowest percent interest on the tax lien that wins the bid. You can see from the examples above, just how low investors are willing to bid down the interest rate depends on the other factors; whether or not there are other penalties, and what interest (if any) is paid on subsequent tax payments.

In other states (like in Maryland and New Jersey) premium is bid for tax liens. As already mentioned, premium is an amount over and above the amount of the tax lien that the investor is willing to pay in order to get the lien. In states where premium is bid, the investor who is willing to bid the highest amount for the lien wins the bid. This also effectively lowers the interest received on the lien. How much your return is decreased by the premium you pay for a lien depends on whether or not you get the premium amount back if the lien redeems, and whether you receive interest or penalties on the premium amount. Some states will pay interest on the premium amount, and as you can imagine premiums are bid up quite high in these states. In New Jersey (remember that in New Jersey the interest rate is bid down, and then premium can be bid) the premium is returned if the lien redeems in 5 years, but without any interest. In addition, some states – like Colorado for instance, premium is not returned to the investor when the lien redeems. Premiums bid at Colorado tax sales are not as high as premiums bid in other states where premium amounts are returned to the investor if the lien redeems.

There are some states in which neither the interest rate nor premium is bid. In these states, one of two other methods can be employed. One of these methods is to bid down the percent ownership of the property. If the lien is not redeemed, and the investor forecloses on the property, they will only have a percent ownership in the property that they bid at the tax sale. In these states, the investor that is willing to accept the lowest percentage of ownership in the property (if the lien does not redeem and they foreclose on the property) wins the bid. This is not very good for investors, and some counties in states that allow for this method of bidding use a random selection process instead.

In the random selection process, investors are randomly offered properties in the tax sale. The plus side of this method is that the investor gets the maximum interest rate that the state allows, and will own 100% of the property if the lien is not redeemed and he or she forecloses the right of redemption. However, the downside is that you have to do your due diligence on all of the properties in the tax sale, because you have no way of knowing which liens you will have a chance to purchase.

**Redemption Period**

The redemption period is the period of time that the owner of the property has to pay the lien. If the lien or redeemable deed is not redeemed during this time, the lien holder can foreclose on the property. Redemption periods vary greatly from state to state and can be as short as six months or as long as three years.

What happens after the redemption period also varies from state to state. In some states, you need to have an attorney foreclose the right to redeem the property. In other states, the investor can petition the court for the deed. In the state of Florida, the lien holder must apply for the property to be sold in a tax deed auction. In the redeemable deed state of Texas, there is nothing that you have to do when the redemption period is over in order to take possession of the property, since as long as the deed was recorded properly; you are already the owner of the property. You will have to clear the title to the property however, but we'll talk about that in a later chapter.

## Expiration Period

This is something that most tax lien investing "experts" don't let you know, but tax liens do expire. Tax liens have different expiration periods in each state. The expiration period can vary anywhere from 6 months after the date of the tax sale to 20 years after the tax sale depending on the state. There is a very big difference in the duration of a tax lien from state to state, and it is important to know the expiration date of a tax lien certificate or redeemable deed. If the investor does not take action to petition for the deed or start foreclosure by the end of the expiration period, the lien can expire worthless.

## Subsequent Taxes

In most states when you purchase a lien, you are paying the prior year's taxes or the taxes from the year before that. Therefore, there may be current taxes that are unpaid. In many states if the property owner doesn't pay the current taxes (known as subsequent taxes), the investor can pay them and get interest on the amount that is paid. Some states will give the statutory (maximum) interest rate on subsequent tax payments. Some of the states in which the interest rate is bid down at the tax sale will only pay the interest rate that was bid at the tax sale on the subsequent tax payments.

Regardless of how much interest you can get on your sub payments, paying them is a way that you can add to your investment without having to bid at the tax sale. How subsequent tax payments are treated in each state is one of the determining factors for how much premium investors are willing to pay for a tax lien or how low in interest they are willing to bid.

## Penalties

Some states have penalties instead of, or in addition to the interest rate. New Jersey is a state that has additional penalties on the certificate amount of 2-6% depending on the amount of the lien. Some municipalities in New Jersey also have a 6% year-end penalty, which is applied to subsequent taxes if the subsequent tax payments are $10,000 or more for any given year. These penalties are in addition to the interest rate. Florida has a 5% redemption penalty instead of the interest if the redemption amount turns out to be less than 5% of the lien amount. Not all states have penalties, but investors are willing to bid higher premiums or bid lower interest rates in the states that do. Some redeemable deed states apply a penalty instead of an annualized interest rate on the bid amount and subsequent tax payments.

When selecting where you are going to invest, you want to keep all of these factors in mind. I always recommend that you check out what happens in your state first, since it is easier to do due diligence on the tax sale properties where you are familiar with the area and property values. Before you can do your due diligence on the tax sale properties however, you have to get the tax sale information and the list of properties in the tax sale. That is exactly what is covered in the next chapter.

# CHAPTER FOUR: Tracking Down the Tax Sale Information

## Finding Out About Tax Sales

The first thing that you need to do once you decide where you want to invest in tax liens or tax deeds is get the tax sale information and the tax sale list, but how do you do that?

One way that you can find out about tax sales in your county is to call the county tax collector or county treasurer and ask for the information about the tax sale. They should be able to tell you when and where the next tax sale takes place, and where you can get a list of properties in the tax sale. Some county treasurers will even have this information posted on their web site along with the rules of the sale and registration guidelines.

Another way to look up county information online and find the county treasurer's or county tax collector's web site is to use the National Association of Counties website (NACO.org). On this site, you can search for a state and get a listing of all of the counties in that state.

When you click on the county link, you can get demographic information for the county and in most cases a link to the county web site where you can search for the county tax collector's and the county tax assessor's information. Some counties have more information online than others do. You might have to be a little bit of a detective to find the information about the tax sale if it is posted online, but you can usually at least find the contact information for the county treasurer so that you can call and get the details about the tax sale.

If you invest in a few different states, you may want to use a tax sale database service that puts all this information at your fingertips and makes it easy for you to find the tax sale information, get the tax sale lists, and do your due diligence on tax sale properties. You'll find some resources for these services at the end of this chapter.

## Getting the Tax Sale List

Once you know when the tax sale is coming up in your area, you need to get the list of properties that are in the sale. I use NACO.org to find tax sale property lists online for tax lien and tax deed sales. This only works for counties that have this information online. For counties or states that do not have information online, you can either call the tax collector and ask how to get the tax sale list or you can buy the tax sale list from a tax sale list provider, like one of the resources mentioned above.

To use NACO.org to get to the county's web site, first go to naco.org and click on the link to find a county. This will bring you to a page with a map of the United States. Click on the state that you are interested in and go to that state's web page to get a list of all the counties in the state. Find the county that you are interested in and click on that link. This will take you to the NACO page for that county. Click on the link to the county on the top of the page and you will go to the county's web site. Note that this will only work if the county has a web site.

Once you are on the county's web site, look for a link to the department or county office that is responsible for conducting the tax sale. For most states, this will be the county treasurer or county tax collector. If you don't know who is responsible for the tax sale in your state, then consult my State Guide. (You can get a free download of my State Guide at TaxLienLady.com/MembershipMain.htm.) Once you get to the web site of the person or department that conducts the tax sale, look for a link to a list of tax sale properties. For larger counties, you can usually find this online.

The exception to this is the counties in the New England states and in New Jersey. Municipal governments - not the counties, conduct tax sales in these states. Instead of looking for the county website or contact information, in Vermont, New Hampshire, Maine, Rode Island, Connecticut, Massachusetts, and New Jersey, look for the municipal tax collector's information to find out details about their tax sales.

**When to Buy the Tax Sale List**

If you can't find the tax sale list that you want online, you can always buy the list from a tax sale list provider. Even if you can find the tax sale list online from the county, you still may want to purchase an enhanced or premium list from a tax sale list provider. That is because the list that you get from the tax collector does not always have the information that you need. Frequently it will only have a parcel ID number, owner's name, and amount due. What you want to know is the address of the property, the assessment data and market value of the property, the property type or class, and the size of the property. All of this (and sometimes even more information) is included in the enhanced or premium lists that you can purchase from a tax sale list provider.

For smaller tax sales you are better off buying a detailed or enhanced list. Since the list is small, you might think that you could save the money and look up all the information that you need yourself. I have found that this process is time consuming and that for small lists I am better off buying the detailed list. It saves me a lot of time in my due diligence; I get all the information that I need, and I only have to go out and look at the properties. Because these lists are smaller than those for the larger tax sales, they cost less.

For larger lists, I would rather do my own research. Detailed tax sale lists that have over 500 properties can cost over $50 and lists that have over 1000 properties can cost over $100. Large counties and big cities can have lists of a few thousand properties and that can cost a few hundred dollars. So how do you decide whether you should buy the detailed list or do the research yourself for these tax sale lists?

Remember that if the original tax sale list has 1000 properties, there will probably be only around 500 properties left on the day of the sale. Since most tax sale list providers do not update the lists that they have for sale, you will have to purchase the detailed information on all 1000 properties even though you will probably only use half of that information.

Here's how I do it. If there is an easy way to get the assessment information that I need, that is if it is available online, I wait until four or five days before the sale, get an updated list from the tax collector, and then I get the assessment information on the properties. To make it even easier, I limit the properties that I research to only those that are in the townships where I want to invest. I may limit my research to only three or four townships in that particular county and to only certain types of properties. If the assessment information is not readily available, I'll buy the detailed list. Some list providers will allow you to filter the list by property type, thus you can buy the list information just on the type of properties that you are interested in bidding on.

## Resources for Tracking Down The Tax Sale Information

**LienSource - LienSource.com** tax sale data and list provider for New Jersey.

**National Association of Counties - NACO.org** lets you find county information and county and municipal websites.

**Tax Sale Resources - TaxSaleResources.com** National tax sale database and tax sale list provider. The image in the beginning of this chapter is a screen shot of the national tax sale search function on their website.

Membership to **Tax Sale Resources** is provided to members of the Tax Lien Profits Accelerator™ (TaxLienLadys Members Area). Find out more about membership to the Tax Lien Profits Accelerator™ at **TaxLienLady.com/Membership.htm**.

# CHAPTER FIVE: Evaluating Tax Sale Properties

I see new investors make the same mistakes repeatedly when determining which properties to bid on. I made these same errors when I first started. In fact, new investors usually make one of these mistakes right from the start. I'm sharing them with you now so that you can avoid them entirely, and so that you will be profitable right from the get go.

**Mistake Number 1: Doing Your Due Diligence Too Early**

New investors are always eager to get started. They frequently want to start researching the tax sale properties right away - as soon as they can get the tax sale list. I also made this mistake when I first started, until I realized that I was wasting my time doing due diligence on properties that were never going to be sold at the tax sale. Not only was I wasting my time, but also I was spending more money than I needed to. I was working for an investor in New Jersey and I had hired and trained people to do due diligence and bid at the tax sales. The problem was that I was paying twice of what I needed to for them to do due diligence on the tax sale properties.

People can pay their taxes and remove their property from the tax sale list, sometimes up until right before the tax sale. Frequently it happens that at least half of the properties that are on the original tax sale list will not be there on the day of the sale. If you start doing due diligence on the tax properties to far ahead of the tax sale, many of the properties that you research will not be in the sale, and you'll be doing due diligence on a lot more properties than you need to. I've learned to wait until a couple days before the tax sale and get an updated list from the tax collector. This way I am only researching the properties that are still on the list a couple of days before the tax sale. If you are going to a very large sale, you might need a week to do your due diligence, but you should not need more time than that.

**Mistake Number 2: Not Doing Enough Due Diligence**

Some new investors are under the false impression that they are guaranteed to get paid on a tax lien certificate. This is simply not true. When tax lien investing "gurus" tout tax liens as being "government guaranteed," what they mean is that the interest rate is set by government law, but it doesn't mean that you are guaranteed to get paid on a tax lien or deed. In fact at the start of most live tax sales there is a disclaimer read to bidders letting them know that it is their responsibility to check out the property before they bid, since the local government does not make any claims about what the property is worth or even that the property indeed exists! The real estate is what guarantees a tax lien or tax deed. Therefore, it is very important to make sure that the property has enough value before bidding on it.

For tax liens this may be as simple as looking at the assessment information on the property and driving by the property to take a look at it. I myself have made the error of bidding on a tax lien based on the assessment information alone and not actually looking at the property. One time I did this and wound up with a tax lien on a shack that was falling apart, and it was right next to a stream. When I finally did look at it, it looked as though if the stream got to high, the fallen down shack would be washed away. Because everything around it was overgrown and it was hard to see from the road, I had a real hard time finding it. My mistake was in not making the extra effort to find it **before** buying the lien. I should have looked at it before I bid.

**Other reasons NOT to bid on a tax lien**

Some time ago one of the subscribers to my web site contacted me with a very "valuable" lien that they wanted to sell. She didn't have the money to foreclose on the lien and wanted either to sell it or partner with someone to foreclose on it. (Have someone else hire a lawyer, pay the subsequent tax payments and foreclosure fees, and share in the profits). When I checked into the property, I found out that it was a vacant piece of land with some value, but the lien holder had already invested more than $16,000.00 into this lien. She had paid subsequent taxes over a few years and when she stopped paying the taxes the lien was struck off to the municipality.

The municipality never foreclosed on the lien either. The original lien had been purchased back in 1993. The municipality picked up the lien in 1997 and the back taxes owed on this property were now approaching the value of the property. The investor could have avoided this situation by doing these three things:

1. Being more particular about the types of properties that she bid on and making sure that the property value was a few times what she bid at the tax sale. (The exact ratio is dependent on whether you are purchasing a lien, deed or redeemable deed and what the state procedures are for foreclosing on tax sale properties.)
2. Paying <u>all</u> the subsequent tax payments.
3. Initiating foreclosure proceedings before the amount of money paid into the investment was more than 30% of the value of the property value.

Here is a list of a few reasons not to buy a tax lien or deed. Unless you know how to deal with these problems, make sure they do not exist on any liens or deeds that you bid on at a tax sale.

- The annual taxes for the property are extremely low (lower than usual for the area)

- You can't find the property on the tax map

- You can't locate the property to look at it

- The property has an unknown owner

- The property is land locked with no right of way

- The property is not large enough or not the right shape to build on (check zoning)

- There are prior tax liens on the property (this does not necessarily rule it out entirely, but requires more research to make sure there is not a reason that another investor has walked away from it)

- The property is or has been contaminated (check the state environmental web site)

- The property is condemned or about to be condemned (eyeball the property or check with the municipality)

- The property is vacant land with a grade that is too steep to build on

- The property is in a flood zone

This is by no means an exhaustive list there are other specific things that you may have to be concerned about in certain areas of the country that are not listed here. You can check for most of them online on the tax assessor's web site and by looking at a GIS map. When it comes to vacant land, however, some things can only be determined by physically looking at the property. There are some things that you can't even tell by looking at the property; like whether or not it will pass a perk test (this is important for rural properties). I recommend that new investors and foreigners stay away from vacant land unless they have someone that can physically look at the property for them.

I provide step-by-step instruction for doing due diligence on tax sale properties in the Build Your Profitable Tax Lien Portfolio home study course. You can find out more about it at ProfitableTaxLienPortfolio.com.

**Six Tips for Doing Due Diligence on Tax Deeds**

You have to be even more rigorous in doing your due diligence for tax deed properties than you do for tax liens because you are actually purchasing the deed to the property at the tax sale. If you make a mistake, there are no refunds, so here are six tips for doing due diligence on tax deed properties.

**1. Get the Property Assessment Record.** You want to get the property record from the tax assessor's office. These records usually show all the information on the property used for valuation, the type of property, the assessed value, and sometimes you can even get the last sale data on the property.

**2. Do a Title Search.** I don't recommend paying a title company to a title search in each of the properties in the tax sale. I do recommend searching the county records yourself (using the owner's name) to find the deed to the property and any liens that exist on the property, or having a title absconder who works in the county recorder's office do it for you.

**3. Look at a GIS map.** GIS stands for Geographic Information Systems and sometimes you can get a GIS map of the property from the property assessor's website. This can show the area that the property is in and Geographic information like whether it's in a flood plain or not.

**4. Get market Value and neighborhood information.** Various websites - like Realtor.com, Zillow.com, and Trulia.com will give you comparisons of nearby properties and allow you to look up demographics about the area. I wouldn't entirely trust their valuations, they usually lag behind the market. However, you could take the lowest market value estimate you get from these sites just to be safe. You can also use these sites to get rental values and demographic information and that affect the value of the properties you're researching.

5. **Find out about possible environmental issues.** Each state has an environmental website that lists known environmental problems. Find the environmental website for the state that you are investing in and locate the list of known problem sites for the county. Do not bid on any properties that are listed as having an environmental issue. You may want to stay away from any properties that are near any of these problem sites as well. A portal that you can use to find public records databases and environmental websites is http://NETROnline.com.

6. **Check Notifications.** You want to check that proper notification of the tax sale has been delivered to the delinquent property owner and all liens holders. One of the reasons for doing a title search is to make sure that all lien holders, as well as the property owner(s) received proper notification of the tax sale. If the property owner or any of the lien holders were not properly notified of the sale, they could contest the sale in court and purchase the property back from you. You would get your money back, but you would have done all that work for nothing.

## Do Liens Survive a Tax Deed Sale?

The other thing that you need to know before you bid on a tax deed is what liens survive the tax sale. This may be different for different states. Even in the same state, there could be different types of tax sales, where different liens survive the sale. In Pennsylvania, for example, many counties have two different tax sales. If you purchase a tax deed in the "upset" tax sale you are responsible for any liens or encumbrances on the property. But in the "judicial" tax sale, the property is sold "free and clear" of any liens (except for government liens). You can see the importance of knowing the rules and knowing which tax sale you are bidding at! Which brings us to step four in our 5 STEPS to buying profitable tax liens: preparing to go to the tax sale.

## Resources for Evaluating Tax Sale Properties

**Build Your Profitable Tax Lien Portfolio** - Step-by-Step online learning program for buying profitable tax liens and tax deeds.
**ProfitableTaxLienPortfolio.com**

**Investor Comps Online** - this is a paid site that gives real comparable data for properties.
**InvestorCompsOnline.com**

**NETRonline.com** - online portal for public records and environmental websites.

**Realtor.com** and **Zillow.com** - for comps and market value of properties.

# CHAPTER SIX: Preparing To Go To the Sale

Now that you've researched the tax sale properties and decided which ones to bid on, it's time to get ready to participate. Preparing to go to the sale consists of registering to bid at the sale along with getting your paperwork and payment in order. In most states, you need to register before the sale in order to bid. Depending on what state and county you are investing in, you may need to register a few weeks before the sale, or you may be able to register a few minutes before it starts. I have been to some tax lien sales in New Jersey and tax deed sales in Pennsylvania where late comers are allowed to register and bid at the tax sale while it is in progress, but that isn't the norm. Some municipalities do not require you to register ahead of time, only that you submit the proper paperwork if you are the successful bidder on a property. In some states, you have to register days or even weeks before the tax sale in order to bid. In Kentucky, you are required to register with the state months ahead of the county sales in order to bid.

Some counties will require a deposit in order to register. The deposit amount could be anywhere from $100.00 to a few thousand dollars (as in the case of many online tax sales). Large deposits are usually returned to the investor if nothing is purchased at the sale. Smaller deposits are sometimes returned and sometimes not returned to the investor, depending on the county. Nassau County, NY, for example, has a tax lien sale in February of each year that typically is 3-4 days long. They have a registration fee of at least $100 for each day that you intend to bid, and the registration fee is non-refundable.

You also need to make sure that you have the proper funds for payment before you go to the sale. For most tax sales, only certified funds are accepted. You need to figure out ahead of time how much money you need. This can be a little difficult because you don't know what properties are going to be left in the sale and you don't know if you will be the successful bidder on any of them. Some tax collectors will allow you time to go the bank to get the funds you need after the sale. If this is the case, you will be able to go to your bank and get a bank check in the exact amount that you need to pay for any liens or deeds that have been awarded to you at the sale. If there is no time allowed to go to the bank, you will have to have the certified funds, made out to the county tax collector, with you at the sale. If you know that this is the case, come up with your best estimate of what you think is the most that you will spend, and have certified checks made up in different denominations that total a little more than you think you'll need. This way if you have to wait for a check from the county for your change, at least it won't be for a very large amount. Make sure you check with the tax collector a couple of days before the sale to find out what the acceptable forms of payment are and whether or not you will be allowed to go to the bank and get a check after the sale.

## Know the rules

The terms of the tax sale are **very** important. They indicate how and when you need to register for the tax sale, what the bidding procedure is, and how and when you need to pay for any successful bids. If you don't provide the proper information, you won't be allowed to register for the tax sale. And, if you don't register by the deadline you won't be allowed to bid. You also need to have the right form of payment, or your payment will not be accepted and you will lose any successful bids and be barred from future sales.

You will need to have certain information with you, or fill out the registration forms ahead of time. For tax lien sales, you will need to complete a W-9 form and a bidder registration form or bidder information sheet. For tax deed sales, you will need to complete a registration form, and you may also need to sign an affidavit stating that you do not owe any taxes in the taxing district or in the county in which you purchase any deeds. For online tax sales, you can register and fill out all of the forms you need online.

Here's a check list that you can use to get ready to bid at your first tax sale. A few days before the tax sale you'll need to accomplish these items:

- **Get the Tax Sale Information**, including the list of properties in the tax sale. (See Chapter 4)

- **Do your research on the tax sale properties** and determine which properties you will bid on. For step-by-step instruction on how to do due diligence on tax sale properties see Chapter 5.

- **Register to bid at the tax sale.** For online tax sales you can do this online but don't wait until right before the tax sale ends. Some counties require you to register a few weeks in advance of the sale (so you might want to this step first). For live tax sales, you may be able to do this right before the tax sale, or a day or two ahead of the auction. Some tax sales have registrations deadlines weeks before the tax sale and others will allow you to register right before it starts, so check this out ahead of time.

- **Determine how much money you will need** if you are the successful bidder on all the properties you plan to bid on at the tax sale. What is the maximum you are willing to spend at the tax sale? Prepare a bidding sheet with the list of tax sale properties that indicates which properties you will bid and how much you will bid. (I use a software program to help with this, see Chapter 10)

- **Secure your funds for the tax sale.** Make sure that you can have your funds on the day of the sale in the acceptable form of payment for that county.

That brings us to the last of our 5 STEPS for buying profitable tax liens - show up and bid at the tax sale. In the next chapter, you'll get some tips for bidding at the sale.

# CHAPTER SEVEN: Bidding At The Tax Sale

You've got the tax sale list and you've done your due diligence and made your preparations to go to the tax sale. You've registered for the sale, you have your paperwork in order, and you've made arrangements to have the proper form of payment. Since most tax sales are auctions, the next step to buying profitable tax liens or tax deeds is to bid at the sale.

Before you bid at a tax sale you need to know what the bidding procedure is and what your strategy will be. You'll have to decide beforehand just how much you are willing to pay for each property that you want to bid on, or how low (in interest or percent ownership) you will bid. I suggest that you attend at least one tax sale before you actually bid at one so that you are aware of how the process works and what the competition is like. It's very important to know exactly what you are bidding.

## What Happens At The Tax Sale?

What happens at the tax sale depends on what state you attend a sale in, and on whether it is a tax lien sale or a tax deed sale. Tax lien sales can be very different from state to state and even from one county to another within a state. Tax deed sales are pretty much the same around the country. At tax deed sales the properties are read off by the auctioneer in the order that they are listed and the price of the property is bid up.

The exception to this is in counties that have online deed sales, like some counties in California and Florida. In order to bid at an online auction, you have to register online and in most cases put down a deposit. The properties are usually listed in batches and a closing time is given for each batch. You submit your bids in on the properties that you want to bid on, but depending on which auction platform is used, you may or may not know who else is bidding and what the other bids are. You may not even know if you are the successful bidder on a property until after the sale is over.

## Bidding Procedures

There are 4 basic types of bidding procedures that are employed at tax lien sales. Usually, either the interest is bid down, the price of the lien is bid up, or the percent ownership in the property is bid down. When the price of the lien or deed is bid up at the tax sale, it is referred to in the tax lien industry as "premium" or "overbid." Different states may refer to it differently and they treat it differently. In some states the amount bid is only the premium or overbid amount, and the total price of the lien will be the bid amount plus the lien amount and other fees – such as an auctioneer's fee, or processing fee, can also be added in. Other states will start the bidding at the lien or deed amount so that the bid price includes the lien amount.

In some states, they do not bid down the interest or bid up the price of the lien. They may use another bidding process in which the percent ownership of the property (should the property be foreclosed) is bid down. In this process, it is the bidder who is willing to receive the lowest percent ownership in the property that wins the bid. Nebraska, Louisiana, and Iowa are tax lien states that use this bidding method. This method is also used in Utah for tax deeds. The percent ownership of the deed is bid down at deed sales in this Utah.

Other bidding procedures that are sometimes used are a random selection or a round robin process (which isn't really bidding at all). In some counties of Iowa and Nebraska, they might use one of these procedures instead of bidding down the percent ownership of the property. In the random selection or round robin process, the interest rate is not bid down and the price is not bid up; they remain constant. In counties that use this process, the successful bidder is randomly selected for each property. In counties that use the round robin procedure, the tax collector will go around the room in a specific order (usually by bidder number), offering the next tax lien to the next registered bidder in line. The bidder can either accept or refuse the lien; but if the lien is refused, another isn't offered until his or her turn comes up again. The chance of getting another lien offered to you may not happen again depending on how many liens, and how many bidders there are.

**Know What You Are Bidding**

It's important to know what you are bidding and what others are likely to bid as well. Newbie investors sometimes think that they will get the maximum bid rate and typically place bids that are too high in interest rate or too low in premium to win the bid. I always suggest that you attend a tax sale first and see what the competition is like. This way you'll know just how much money you need if premium is bid, and whether this tax sale is worth your time or not. When I'm working with one of my students, one of the first things we do is look at the results of past tax sales to see just what they need to pay to be successful and whether or not it's worth it to attend a particular tax sale.

There are so many different bidding procedures that you really need to know what you are bidding at any particular tax sale. You need to know what is bid; is it the interest rate, ownership interest in the property, or premium. If you are bidding premium, what happens to it? Do you get interest on your premium? Do you even get your premium back if the lien redeems? This could make a big difference in how much you profit when the lien redeems.

**Avoid Newbie Mistakes**

Another mistake that newbie investors make is getting carried away at the auction and paying too much premium, or bidding too low in interest. Always know what your bottom line is – what is the lowest interest rate you are willing to accept and what is the most you are willing to pay for the property - and don't go beyond your predetermined amount!

I was at a tax sale in New Jersey where a new investor bid $1000 premium on a small $200 tax lien. The lien was a utility lien (utility liens are also sold at tax sales in some states and are treated the same as a tax lien), and all of the tax payments were current. That means that the investor would not be able to pay any subsequent taxes, only subsequent utilities (in this case it was a sewer lien) which are much smaller amounts. If the lien redeems after the redemption period the investor will get back their $1000.00 premium – with no interest or penalties along with the redemption amount. Even if she gets to pay $500.00 per year in subsequent sewer amounts, she would receive back the certificate amount with a 2% penalty, but no interest (which is only $4.00) and get only 8% interest on the subsequent payments. (only when the property owner is $1500 delinquent do you get 18% on your sub payments in NJ) Her entire profit would be only $44, but she invested a total of $1700 over 2 years, with more than half of it invested right in the beginning. That's a yield of a little more than 2.5% over 2 years - probably not what she was expecting!

In this case the investor did not know that she wasn't going to receive any interest on the premium that she bid, or on the certificate amount. She really didn't know what she was doing, but she kept bidding because other investors were also bidding. Sometimes seasoned investors continue bidding because they want to bid new investors up to the point where it is not profitable for them. They think that by doing this they will discourage newcomers from coming back. Then there are the institutional bidders that need to place a certain amount of money per year, so sometimes they pay more than they should for liens. Don't let them bid you up to numbers that don't make any sense.

## Tips for Bidding at the Tax Sale

Here are some tips for bidding at tax sales to help you increase your chances of winning bids at a live tax lien or tax deed auction.

- Get to the tax sale early so that you can get a good seat and check on last minute updates (properties are always coming off the tax sale list right before the sale starts).

- Bring any paper work that you need for the tax sale; bidder registration, w-9 form, and bidder number if you've been issued one beforehand.

- Bring your own bid sheet listing the tax sale properties with the items that you want to bid on indicated, along with the lowest interest rate or highest premium that you are willing to bid.

- Have your funds for payment available.

- Make sure that you're seated in plenty of time before the sale begins, it's better to get a good seat where the auctioneer can easily see you.

- Turn off your cell phone; any distraction once the auction begins can cost you a bid.

- Pay for any liens or deeds that you win by the deadline, or you will lose any successful bids, and be barred from future sales.

## What About The Competition?

Tax lien investing is not the best-kept secret in America. It may have been 20 years ago, when only the wealthy knew about it, but the secret is out now. Because of the insecurity in the economy and the stock market, fund managers are now looking to diversify their investments with tax liens. In some areas of the country, this is putting a squeeze on investors. In addition, there are constantly new investors coming into the game that don't know what they are doing and bid premium amounts that are too high or interest rates that are too low to be profitable. So how do you stay ahead of the competition at tax sales?

The first thing that I have my clients do in order to find out about the competition and how much money they will need to be a successful bidder, is to check out the results of previous tax sales. What happened at last year's tax sale? There is no guarantee that what happened last year will repeat itself this year, but at least you can tell what is likely to happen. You can also look at what the trend has been over the last few years and get a feel for what this year's sale might be like.

Then I take a look at the types of properties that are heavily bid at the sales and the types of properties that don't get many bids. I try to concentrate on the type of properties that the institutional buyers don't want. There usually are many bids on the pretty, residential properties, because investors think that these properties are likely to redeem. Most of the funds and banks that invest in tax liens are looking for redemptions, not a chance to foreclose on the property, so they go after these types of properties. Residential properties that may need a lot of work, and vacant land may not get as many bids. These are the properties that I would target.

Keep in mind that the easier a tax sale is to get to and the more desirable the area, the more competition there is likely to be. I go to smaller rural areas and stay out of the big cities, and nicer suburban areas. Even though there is more available in the bigger cities and less available in the rural areas, the competition is usually not as fierce.

## What About Leftovers?

In the last couple of years there have been a few real estate investing and wealth building "experts" that suggest that bidding at the tax sale is too competitive and that you can get much better deals when buying leftover liens or deeds directly from the county. These are tax lien certificates or tax deeds that did not sell at the tax sale. No one bid on them at the sale and they were struck off to the county, state, or municipality. A few states allow the assignment of these leftover or "over-the-counter" (OTC) tax lien certificates or tax deeds to investors. There are pros and cons to purchasing leftover or assignment liens or deeds from the county.

On the positive side, there is no competition; you don't have to bid against other investors. You may even be able to purchase a lien or redeemable deed in which the redemption period has already ended, or is close to being over, in which case you may be able to foreclose on the property. For some deed states, since the county, state, or municipality has already taken title to the property, you may not have to go through a title clearing process (quiet title or title certification process).

On the negative side, OTC liens and deeds are seldom worth bidding on in the first place and that's why they were not sold at the tax sale. Think about it; most counties that have online tax sales will have a second tax sale (sometimes called the cleanup sale) where they sell everything that didn't sell in the first tax sale. Only after this sale does a property then get on the OTC list. If tax sales are so competitive that these experts say you can't get a good deal at the tax sale, what makes you think there is anything good leftover?

In smaller counties and in states where the tax sales are conducted by the municipality (New Jersey, and the New England states) there is usually nothing worthwhile that is left over. To find leftover tax liens or deeds, you have to go to counties that have very large lists (a few thousand properties) to begin with. And you have to sift through a lot of junk to find good properties.

## Are OTC Liens & Deeds Deals or Duds?

Yes, you can get the maximum interest rate, when you purchase an OTC lien and you can buy OTC deeds without bidding up the price at the tax sale. And yes, you will probably be able to get the property - in which case you do not get your money back, you get the property instead. But how are you going to sell an unbuildable piece of land, or otherwise junk property and get your money out of your investment?

Sometimes a good property does get onto the OTC list, but it's usually not because it didn't get any bids in the tax sale. Sometimes bidders don't have the proper form of payment, or don't pay up by the deadline. In that case, the property will go onto the leftover list. There are plenty of investors, however, who wait until this list is available and buy these properties right away. Since properties on this list are offered on a first come, first serve basis, the early bird gets the worm. The juicy worms are pretty much gone by daybreak!

There are investors who do well using this strategy, but it is not a strategy that I teach to beginners. It is very time intensive. You really have to do your research carefully if you want a deal and not a dud. The best way to work this strategy is to be at the tax sale and note which tax liens are not sold, and then get that leftover list as soon as it is published and take action immediately. This way you will know what properties are likely to be on the list from the last sale that are good properties and not junk, and you can do your due diligence on these properties ahead of time. Then as soon as the list is available, you can make your purchase right away.

Sometimes you can find a nugget of gold in the leftover tax sale list. I know a couple of tax lien investors in Arizona who do this regularly as well as a couple of tax deed investors (in Texas and Pennsylvania) who have done this. With more and more people becoming interested in tax lien and tax deed investing and going to the auctions, there are not as many leftover liens and deeds as there used to be. My advice is to use extreme caution and be extremely rigorous with your due diligence when purchasing leftover liens or deeds. I also believe that investing long distance in leftover liens or deeds is a mistake if you do not have someone that can physically look at the property for you.

# PART II Managing Your Portfolio

# CHAPTER EIGHT: Protecting Your Profit

Once you purchase profitable tax liens or tax deeds, you want to protect your investment and maximize your return. Depending on whether you are investing in liens or deeds and which state you are investing in, the steps you will take to do this may include the following:

- Recording your lien or deed with the county clerk
- Paying subsequent taxes
- Clearing the title to the property
- Foreclosing the right to redeem a tax lien or redeemable deed

**Recording Your Lien or Deed**

Regardless of whether you purchased a tax lien, a tax deed, or a redeemable tax deed, the first thing that you will need to do is record your lien or deed with the county clerk. This is not necessary for tax liens in every state, but in some states unless the lien is recorded, all you have is a worthless piece of paper. (There are states, like Arizona and Florida, which do not require you to record a tax lien). For tax deeds, the deed always has to be recorded. In some states, this is done for you and you will be charged a recording fee when you purchase your tax deed at the tax sale. In many states though, it is the investor's responsibility to do this and you are given a specific time frame in which it needs to be done. In some redeemable deed states, like Texas for example, the redemption period does not start until the deed is recorded, so you'll want to do that right away. It is to your advantage to check out ahead of time what the procedures and laws are in your state for recording a tax lien or tax deed.

If you do need to record your lien or deed I suggest that you do it right away. You'll have to wait until you have the deed or tax lien certificate, then you will have to send the original document, along with the recording fee, to the proper office to be recorded with the county records. The required fee will vary depending on the state and county. You will need to call the recording office (usually the county clerk, or county recorder) and find out what the fee is so that you can send the exact amount in with the document. If you do not send the right amount, your lien or deed will be returned to you without being recorded.

I suggest that you make a copy of the tax lien certificate or deed before you send it to the county clerk for recording, and that you send it via certified mail, with a return receipt. This way if your document is lost, (which has happened to an investor I know) you have proof that you sent it in to be recorded and you may be able to get it replaced. Keep in mind that the recording process can take some time, and if anything happens with the property in the meantime, at least you'll have a copy of the document.

Once the lien or deed is recorded, it will be sent back to you. Put it in a safe place. In the states in which the investor holds the certificate, you will not be able to receive the redemption without handing over the signed document to the tax collector. Do not sign it and turn it over to the tax collector until you are sure that the redemption amount is the amount that is due to you. To ensure that your tax payments, recording fees and other reimbursable expenses are returned to you upon redemption, you will have to provide the tax collector with an affidavit for any payments that you make on your tax lien. That brings us to the next thing you need to do to protect your investment and maximize your return– pay the subsequent taxes.

## Paying Subsequent Taxes

When you purchase a tax lien, some states will allow you to pay the current unpaid taxes (remember that the taxes you paid in order to get the lien are most likely the prior year's taxes) and any subsequent taxes that the property owner hasn't paid. I recommend that you pay the subsequent taxes (referred to as "subs"), if your state allows it, as soon as possible. Some states will give you the maximum interest on your subs and some will only give you the interest that you bid at the sale, but most states that allow you to pay the subs also give you interest on the subsequent tax payments when the lien redeems. This is one way that you can maximize your profit in a tax lien.

When you purchase a tax deed, the property is now yours and you must pay the subsequent taxes or the property will go into next year's tax sale. Redeemable deed states vary as to how they handle the subsequent tax payments. In some states, you are obligated to pay them and in others, you do not pay the subsequent taxes until the redemption period is over and you are the owner of the property.

Whenever you make a subsequent tax payment, you'll need to submit an affidavit to the tax collector to prove that you paid them. Some states will even have a special form that you need to fill out whenever you make a subsequent tax payment or pay for other reimbursable expenses for the lien or deed. You will have to inquire from the tax collector what the subsequent tax amount is and when it has to be paid. Many counties will only accept subsequent tax payments at certain times of the year, and some will only allow you to request to pay them at certain times.

**Take the Sub Way to Profit!**

A few years ago one of my tax liens redeemed that I had held since 2002. The reason that I'm telling you about this particular redemption is that it proves a point about the importance of paying subsequent taxes. I made over $3,200 in profit on that lien, with an investment of a little more than $4,000. Here is the 1099 interest form that I received from the municipality and the statement for the check that I received to prove it:

I had put that money into this lien over the course of 7 years and then did nothing for 3 more years. During that time, the money I had invested kept earning interest. My initial investment was only around $450 and I kept adding to that each year for the first 7 years, paying the subsequent taxes (in this case it was a utility lien so I was paying the subsequent utility payments). Then I decided to force redemption by sending a pre-foreclosure letter to the owners and lien-holders of the property. The mortgage holder then paid off the lien, and I practically doubled my money – investing a little each year. I didn't even go to the tax sale for those years that I paid the subsequent taxes. All I had to do to add to my investment was call or fax the tax collector to request what the subsequent payment amounts were, and send in the payment with an affidavit.

You can't let your liens go this long in every state because some states have shorter expiration periods, but I did this in New Jersey where you earn the statutory rate (18%) on most of your subsequent tax payments and the lien does not expire for 20 years. Most states do have shorter expiration periods and not all states give the maximum interest that the state allows on sub payments.

Remember that the laws are different in every state, so before you try any of these strategies, make sure that you check the state statutes regarding the redemption of tax lien certificates, or check with a tax lien attorney in your state.

## Clearing the Title

When you buy a tax deed at a tax sale, you are likely to get a non-warrantee deed for the property. That means that there is no warrantee as to the condition of the title to the property. You are buying the property without clear title (inheriting a title problem) and if you want to resell it to someone who will need financing you will need to clear the title.

Very few states issue a warrantee deed at a tax sale. You can clear the title to the property in one of two ways. You can either hire an attorney to do a lengthy and expensive quiet title court process where you file suit to anyone who had an interest in the property at the time of the tax sale or you could hire a title company to do a title certification process. Which process is best to use will depend on the state. I do recommend that if you use an attorney that you find one that does a lot of this type of work and is experienced with tax title deeds.

You could also use a company that specializes in tax title clarification. Tax Title Services is a national company that specializes solely in servicing the title on tax deed and foreclosed tax lien properties. They have developed a qualification process that enables tax lien/deed investors to obtain title insurance on their tax-deeded properties through their program title underwriters without the need to file quiet title actions or to wait out statute of limitation periods. They are faster and normally cheaper than most attorneys that do this work.

## Foreclosing the Right of Redemption

If you purchase a tax lien and it is not redeemed during the redemption period, than you may need to foreclose the right to redemption on the property in order to get paid. In my experience, this happens very seldom, but when it does, you will need an attorney to handle this for you. It may seem like a simple process, but there are many steps that have to be followed exactly or you could lose your right to the property. I also recommend that you only use an attorney who specializes in tax lien foreclosures. Attorneys who specialize in this area are familiar with the difficulties that come up and know how to handle them. Because they are very familiar with the process, they will be able to get through it faster than an attorney who does not do many tax lien foreclosures.

Not all states require a judicial foreclosure; some only require that you apply through the courts for the deed. In some redeemable deed states, like Texas, for example, the deed is already recorded in your name and when the redemption period is over, you are the owner of the property. Florida also differs from other lien states in that if the lien does not redeem, you don't get to foreclose on the property. Instead, you have to apply for the lien to go to a deed sale, where it will be sold at a tax deed auction in order to satisfy the tax lien.

In the next chapter, you'll learn more about what happens when your lien or redeemable deed redeems, and about the foreclosure process. You'll also learn about a third way that you can profit on your tax lien or redeemable deed.

> **Chapter Resources**
>
> **Tax Title Services** – is a national company that specializes solely in servicing the title on tax deed and foreclosed tax lien properties. You can find out more about how they can help you clear the title to your tax sale property at **TaxLienInvestingTips.com/?p=3666**.

# CHAPTER NINE: Cashing In On Your Investment

## Three Ways to Profit

There are three ways that you can profit from your tax lien or redeemable deed:

1. The lien or deed redeems and you collect your principal plus interest and/or penalties
2. The property owner does not redeem the lien or deed within the redemption period and you get the property. (In some states, you will have to foreclose the right of redemption first).
3. You can sell or "assign" your lien or redeemable deed to another investor.

## Redemption

You don't get paid on your tax lien or redeemable deed until the owner of the property decides to redeem the lien. When this happens, there are procedures that the property owner has to follow. In most states, the redemption is accomplished through the tax collector. The property owner will contact the tax collector (or county treasurer) and get the redemption amount. The property owner must pay the amount the investor paid for the lien or deed, any subsequent tax payments that were made, plus any interest, penalties and allowed expenses. **(Important note: not all states return the premium so check this out before you invest!)**

Depending on the county, the tax collector may notify you and verify the redemption amount with you first, or they may just accept payment from the property owner, and send you a redemption check. If you have a lien or redeemable deed from a county where you hold the certificate or deed, then you have somewhat of an upper hand. The lien on the property will not be released (and you not be paid) until you surrender the signed certificate or deed. Don't do this until you agree with the amount that is owed to you.

**Note: If you are holding the tax lien certificate or deed, the tax lien certificate must be turned into the tax collector, usually signed and notarized before you receive the redemption. It's very important to keep the tax lien certificate or redeemable deed in a safe place. Although most states allow for replacement of these documents it may cost you time and money to replace a lost document.**

I use a software program that will calculate the redemption amount for me. When one of my liens redeems, the tax collector will call or send me a fax, giving me the redemption amount and ask if I agree. I can run a redemption report on my software and if my numbers are close to the tax collector's amount, then I will agree and send in the signed certificate. If my report does not agree with what the tax collector says I should receive, then I go back and check my records to see if there is anything that they forgot to account for. It has happened more than once that the tax collector failed to add in one of my subsequent tax payments. They will then correct the error and notify the property owner, or whoever is redeeming the lien (in many cases it is the bank or mortgage company), of the right amount necessary for the redemption of the lien.

It is important to send in an affidavit whenever you make a subsequent tax payment so that you have proof that you made each payment. Make sure that you keep a copy as well. The software I use generates an affidavit for me whenever I send in a payment for subsequent taxes, record a lien, or pay foreclosure expenses. I then will have the tax collector stamp it with their signature and send a copy back to me. Then I have proof that they received it. I also keep an original copy, in case they don't send it back to me. You'll learn more about automating your investing with tax lien software in the next chapter, but let's move on to find out what happens when your lien doesn't redeem and you have to foreclose.

## What if Your Lien Doesn't Redeem?

I just love it when I get checks in the mail from tax collectors for redemptions of my tax liens. Nevertheless, what do you do when your liens don't redeem and the redemption period is over? This is somewhat state specific because some states do not give you much time to foreclose once the redemption period is over. You may only have 6 months after the redemption period before the lien expires, in those states you will have to start the foreclosure or deed application process right away.

In states where tax liens have longer expiration periods there are things that you can do to maximize your return on your investment and get paid when you want to. Since I invest in a state that has a 2 year redemption period and a 20 year expiration period, I can let my liens go way past the redemption period and not worry about losing my investment as long as I pay the subsequent taxes. In fact the more I let the lien ride and pay my subsequent taxes, the more money I'll make. But there does come a time when I have more money into the lien than I want to have. I don't want the redemption amount to approach the value of the property; I don't want it to come close to half of the value of the property. I prefer it to be less than 30% of what the property is worth.

So how do you know when it's time to start foreclosure on a property and force redemption, and how do you know if the property will redeem or if you will actually get to foreclose on it? If there is a mortgage or other substantial interest in the property, other than the homeowner, the lien is likely to redeem after you send out notices of the intent to foreclose. The property owner was not able to pay the taxes, and likely will not be able to redeem the lien. However, a mortgage holder, once they have notice of a probable tax lien foreclosure, will most likely redeem the lien to protect their interest in the property.

Here are some other reasons why you may want to start the foreclosure process to force redemption on a tax lien, other than the redemption amount becoming more than 30% of the value of the property:

- You did not pay the subsequent taxes for whatever reason and someone else bought a subsequent tax lien on the property and now their redemption period is almost over.

- You are concerned that the owner of the property may be entering bankruptcy.

- You need cash

Foreclosure procedures vary from state to state and in some states, they can be expensive and take a long time, especially now that the courts are filled with so many bank foreclosures around the country. In many states this is a judicial process where you 'foreclose the right to redeem' the lien or redeemable deed. For this process it is best to use a tax lien attorney, who knows the ins and outs of the process.

In other states, you may have to petition the court for the deed. In Florida, you must apply for the lien to be auctioned in a deed sale. In Texas, you automatically receive the property when the redemption period is over. (The redeemable deed is already recorded, and is validated when the redemption period is over).

The first step in the foreclosure process to perform a title search on the property and send notification to all parties that have an interest in the property – the owner and all liens holders. What has to be included in the notification, and who needs to be notified is regulated by the state statutes and needs to be followed exactly. In most states, an attorney handles this step, and the rest of the foreclosure process. What happens next is state specific, so I won't go into that here.

What I do want to talk about next is what you can do if the redemption period isn't over yet, and you want to get the cash out of your investment. You can't send an 'intent to foreclose' letter if the redemption period isn't over yet, but you can send a notice of the lien to any lien holders on the property. (**Note:** check with the laws in your state first, in some tax lien states it may be illegal to contact the owner or lien holders before the redemption period is over). If there is a mortgage on the property and they are notified of your lien, there is a good chance that they will redeem it. Here is another instance where you will need to do a title search to find out if there are any lien holders that you can send notices to. You just need a simple title search, and you may even be able to do it yourself, by searching the public records online, or by going to the county Hall of Records.

**Assignment of Your Lien or Deed**

Another way to get your profit and principal out of your investment before the redemption period is over is to sell or "assign" your lien to another investor. Most states do allow for assignment of your lien or redeemable deed to another investor. When you assign or sell your lien or redeemable deed to another investor, you have no more right to the redemption of the lien or redeemable deed, nor do you have any right to foreclose or to pay the subsequent taxes. That right is 'assigned' to the entity or person that you sell your lien or redeemable deed to. However, you can charge any price you want for your lien or deed.

I suggest that you sell it for the 'face amount' of the lien which is the amount that your lien or deed would redeem for. You may want to sell if for less than that if you are anxious to get your cash out now, but make sure that you still make a profit. If there are problems with the property, however, and you just want out, you may have to sell it at a discount.

In order to assign your lien to another investor you need to prepare an assignment contract. The contract should list the buyer and seller, the buyers address, the amount of consideration for the lien or deed (this is how much money you are selling for), the date of the assignment, as well as the particulars for the lien or deed, both the property information and the certificate information. This should include the following:

- Tax ID number
- Block and lot
- Street address
- City & state where the property resides
- Property owner
- Tax lien certificate number or deed number
- Date of Issue
- Name of the tax collector or county treasurer that issued the certificate or deed
- Taxing jurisdiction
- County in which it is recording
- County records book and page number where the document is recorded

You will also need a place for the signature of the seller and notarization of the document.

Assignment is also another way you can buy tax liens or redeemable deeds. You can read about that strategy in Chapter 13. In the next chapter, you'll learn more about automating the process of tax lien investing with specialized software.

# CHAPTER TEN: Automating Your Investing

You've learned from the previous chapters that there are certain things that you need to do in order to keep your investment in tax liens or tax deeds profitable. By automating your business with tax lien software, you won't miss any deadlines that might reduce your profit on your tax lien or tax deed portfolio. You must keep track of when you bought your tax lien certificate, or redeemable deed, when subsequent tax payments are due, when the redemption period ends, and when your liens expire. You will also need a system for recording liens with the county, sending out foreclosure notices at the end of the redemption period, sending out requests to tax collectors for taxes due and tracking the profitability of your liens.

Let's start from the beginning. Before you even purchase a tax lien certificate, you need to contact the tax collector and get a list of the sale properties. Some tax collectors will give you a list with all the information that you need to do your due diligence, but most will not. You need a system for finding the information that you need, doing due diligence on the properties and keeping track of which properties you want to bid on and just how much you can pay and still make a decent profit.

I use a software program to help me with all of this and I am able to download the tax sale lists right into my software. It also has all of the contact information that I need including the phone numbers and addresses of all of the tax collectors in the state that I invest in. If I buy a list from a tax sale provider, like Tax Sale Resources or LienSource, I can import all the data directly into my software program. The software has its own calendar that will show all the tax sales that I import, as well as relevant dates for any of the liens I own, such as when taxes are due and when redemptions periods are over.

The Software allows me to print a due diligence sheet that lists the tax sale properties. I can take this form with me when I look at the properties. It calculates how much premium, if any, I can pay for the properties on the list based on my bottom line. It also allows me to print out a bid sheet listing all the properties in the order that they are offered at the sale, and I can indicate the maximum price or minimum interest rate that I can pay for each property so that I know when to stop bidding. This way the emotion of the auction does not carry me away and I make sure that I am profitable. This is very important in states where the bidding is very competitive.

After I purchase liens at a tax sale, I use the software to track my liens. I keep track of all of my expenses, like recording the lien, and any subsequent tax payments made. I can also print out an affidavit to send to the tax collector with my subsequent tax payments with one click of my mouse. This is very important, because without an affidavit, I could lose any additional payments and the interest accrued on them. I can also use the software to track my current profit to date on any individual lien or my entire portfolio and it will let me know when I need to pay subsequent taxes and when a lien is ready to foreclose. I can even track the progress of the foreclosure.

The program I use is Tax Lien Manager™. It is customized software and is currently only available for these five tax lien states:

- Arizona
- Florida
- Indiana
- Nassau County, NY
- New Jersey

And the redeemable deed state of South Carolina.

You can find out more about Tax Lien Manager™ software at www.TaxLienLady.com/TLM.

If you are investing in other states there is a simple tracking software available that works for every state. The name of that software program is Tax Lien Portfolio Tracker and you can find out more about it and get a free demo trial at www.TaxLienLady.com/Software.htm.

**Time Verses Money**

Using software to automate the business of tax lien investing is one way to save time and money. After all, your time is worth money. I find that Newbie investors either have a lot of money to invest and no time to do it, or plenty of time to invest but not a lot of money. If you fall into the first category of having a considerable amount to invest, but no time to learn how to do it, let alone do the necessary due diligence and go to tax sales, then you really want to pay attention to the next chapter.

# PART III More Ways to Invest

# CHAPTER ELEVEN: Done For You Investing

**Have Money But No Time?**

Some people have plenty of money to invest in tax liens or tax deeds, but no time to do the due diligence and bid at the tax sales. If you're short on time but you have a substantial amount of money to invest, then you might want to use a tax lien agent or a tax lien investing fund to do the work for you.

Although buying tax liens online is a way that you can participate in tax sales without going to the sale, you still have to spend the time to do your due diligence. What if you could give your money to someone else, who could do all the work, bid at the tax sale for you, and manage your portfolio? What if you didn't have to do anything except collect your profit? There are ways that you can invest in tax liens or tax deeds without doing any of the work. You can invest in a tax lien fund, or with a tax lien or tax deed agent. So how do these two methods of investing work and which is best for you?

**Double Digit Returns Without Doing The Work**

Agents and fund managers are experts at purchasing and managing profitable tax liens and tax deeds for their clients. They have a competitive edge over individual investors, and they have a better chance of getting profitable liens than you do. By using a tax lien or tax deed agent or investing in a tax lien fund, you not only eliminate the problem of not having enough time to do the work; you also manage to be more competitive.

Investing with an agent or in a fund also solves the problem of having to travel to participate in tax sales that are not in your home state. For instance if you live in California, which is a deed state but you want to invest in tax liens, that could be a problem if you're doing it yourself, but not if you invest in a fund or with an agent. Investing in a fund or through an agent is also more convenient for foreigners who want to buy US tax liens and deeds (see the next chapter).

If someone else does all the work, you will have to compensate them for their services, so there is a trade-off. It will cost you a little bit of your profit to have someone else do the work for you. How much you pay for this service depends on how much money you invest and whether you invest in a fund or through an agent.

## Tax Lien Investing Agent

With a tax lien investing agent, you have a little more control over your portfolio than with a fund. Sometimes you can actually stipulate what type of properties or liens you want, and control whether or not you pay the subsequent taxes, foreclosure on a property, or sell your lien to another investor. You also have control over whether any profit that you realize gets re-invested. Tax lien certificates and tax deeds are held in your name, so they are your assets. The agent will set up an account for you and assign the liens and/or deeds that they purchase to you after they acquire them the tax sale.

Most agents require a minimum investment of $20,000 or $30,000 and they take an upfront fee that can be 6-15% of your initial investment in addition to maintenance fees. One of the agents that I recommend to my students charges 8% per year on actively placed funds. However, their average return to investors (before fees) has been 30%. If you get to foreclose on a property, the agent will take 25% of your profit on the property. (The standard for the industry is anywhere from 25% to 50%).

## Tax Lien Investing Funds

When you invest in a tax lien fund, you have no control over which tax liens or deeds are purchased and whether or not the profit is re-invested, this is all dictated by the fund. The plus side is that since you are buying shares in a fund, and not investing through your own private account, there are usually no set up fees. There is a management fee but for smaller funds, these fees are typically low.

When you invest in a fund, you are buying shares in the fund, not individual liens or deeds. All of the assets are held in the fund and not in your name. There is no upfront set up fee as there may be when you invest through an agent. When profit is realized by the fund, the proceeds are split evenly among shareholders. Because the expenses are shared by all of the shareholders in the fund, fees tend to be lower than when using an agent. Fees for one of the smaller private funds that I have personally invested in are 3.5% per year, and the fund manager will take a bonus of 25% of any profit from properties that are foreclosed on. These fees are shared by all the members.

**The Competitive Advantage**

The bigger players have a huge advantage over the individual investor, especially at the online auctions. Some of the online auctions allow bidders to have sub-accounts, but you must have a tax ID number for each sub-account. That means that these huge funds can use the social security numbers of all of their members and have hundreds, or even thousands of bids on one property. If there is more than one bid at the lowest interest rate, the winner is chosen randomly. By having a large number of bids on any lien, the institutional buyers increase their chances of winning the bid - especially compared to the individual investor who doesn't have any sub-accounts. So instead of competing with these companies, why not give one of them your money and share in the profits?

That is essentially what you do when you buy into a tax lien investing fund. There are a couple of drawbacks however, to investing in the larger tax lien funds. First, they usually have a very large minimum investment $50,000 - $100,000, and second, their management fees can be quite high, like typical hedge fund fees, and cut into your rate of return.

## Private Investment Funds

A few years ago I stumbled onto a private tax lien investing Fund Company. This company is small enough that it doesn't have a huge minimum investment or inflated fees. They also have a proven track record. I invested in one of their funds in 2008 and then I invested in another of their funds in 2010. I've been recommending them to my members and coaching clients ever since. They have a new fund offering only once a year.

Each new fund is capped at 2.5 million dollars. That means that once they reach that amount they close the fund to any new investors. There is also a closing date for the fund, and even if they don't reach their maximum capital investment amount, the manager will close the fund to new investors after the closing date.

Each new fund usually has an investment horizon of 6-7 years with targeted double-digit annualized returns over the life cycle of the fund. There are a limited number of unaccredited investor's spots (35); available on a first come, first served basis once the fund is opened to new investors.

One of the advantages to being a member of the Tax Lien Profits Accelerator™ (Tax Lien Lady's Members Area), or of being in one of my coaching programs, is that you get to find out when one of these new funds opens before the general public. Since I am an investor of previous funds, I am one of the first to find out when a new fund is started – and I relay this information first to my members and active students and then to my subscribers. Because this fund company has many happy customers that re-invest with them, there are never many spots available for very long, so it's important to act on the opportunity when it arises.

You can find out more about membership to the Tax Lien Profits Accelerator™ and all benefits that go along with it at www.TaxLienLady.com/Membership.htm.

## Why Invest with an Agent or Fund?

Agents and fund managers have a lot of experience purchasing tax liens and tax deeds at the sale. They know the buying strategies that make the most sense and they have an interest in getting the highest returns for their clients. They can usually do better than you can at the tax sale – win more liens at more profitable rates. They have a team set up to research the tax sale properties, and they have access to resources that you might not have access to, hence they are better able to get more liens or deeds and at better returns than you could on your own. They are professionals after all; this is their job, it is what they do for a living, and they're very good at it. It would cost you more to have access to the services and resources that they have access to because they are giving a lot of business to the professionals they work with. The extra money that it would cost you to pay for legal services, title services, and other services and resources you need to research, foreclose, and manage tax sale properties on your own make it worth your while to pay the management fees.

## Investing with an Agent or Fund is Ideal for Foreign Investors

Investing with an agent or in a fund is a great way for foreigners to invest in US tax liens or deeds. The process is easier because you have a U.S. entity bidding for you. You still would need to have a U.S. tax ID number, but you wouldn't always need to have a U.S. bank account, (depending on the agent or fund you invest with) which is a requirement for all of the online tax sales. In addition, you can avoid having to go to through the trouble and expense of setting up a U.S. entity just to bid at the tax sale, although you still may want to have an entity to hold any properties that you acquire through tax sales.

For more information on how foreigners can invest in US tax liens and tax deeds from afar see the next chapter.

# Chapter 11 Resources

**PIP-Group (Platinum Investment Properties - Group)** - Established in 2004 as PIP-West, is a Servicing Agent for purchasing and managing conservative high yield investments including tax liens and tax deeds. Their minimum investment for Illinois Tax Liens is $25,000 and the minimum investment to have them purchase redeemable tax deeds for you in South Carolina, or Georgia is $50,000.

**Texas Tax Sale Resources Group** – Tax deed investing agent for redeemable deed investing in the state of Texas.

**Bonus – Get the replays of webinar recordings with Charles Sells of PIP Group and Arnie Abramson of Texas Tax Sale Resources Group along with other valuable bonuses when you go to http://TaxLienInvestingSecrets.com/freebookbonuses and input your name, email address and receipt number from the purchase of this book.**

# CHAPTER TWELVE: Investing From Afar

What if you have the time and the money to invest, but you live far enough away from where you plan on investing that travel expenses cut deeply into your profit. For foreigners, it simply is not worth it to travel to the U.S. to invest in tax liens or tax deeds, unless you have a quite a bundle to invest. If you live far from where you want to invest, you can invest online, but there are some considerations for online investing you should know about.

**Investing In Tax Liens Online**

Many new tax lien investors are attracted to the idea of investing in tax liens online. They want to be able to purchase tax liens from their computer without having to attend a physical tax sale auction. It's easy to register and bid at the online tax sales and many counties also have resources for you to research the properties online as well.

**So How Do You Get Started?**

More counties are starting to conduct their tax sales online each year. Almost all of the counties in Florida have online tax lien sales, and about half of the Arizona and Colorado counties have online tax sales as well. The States of Indiana and Maryland currently have at least a few counties that have online tax lien sales. The state of Louisiana has many Parishes with online tax lien and tax deed sales (although they have different names for them). More and more New Jersey municipalities are conducting online tax sales each year. Douglas County Nebraska has had an online tax lien sale for the last few years. Just a couple of years prior to the writing of this book, 5 Iowa counties had their first online tax lien sales, and now it seems that more Iowa counties are having their tax sale online each year.

Some deed states also have tax sales online. Most of the counties in the states of California and Michigan have online tax sales and there a few counties in Florida and in Indiana that have online tax deed sales as well. (Florida and Indiana have both tax lien and tax deed sales.) Some of the counties in New York also have online tax deed sales.

Once you find out which counties have online tax sales, go to the tax sale web site and read all of the information about the tax sale. Make sure that you understand when you need to register, how to bid, and what your responsibilities are as a bidder at the tax sale. You'll need to know when and how you are expected to pay for successful bids and whether or not you'll need to have a deposit wired ahead of time in order to bid at the tax sale.

Find out what information is available on the tax sale web site or on the county's web site for researching the properties that are in the tax sale. Can you download the tax sale properties in an excel file that has all the information that you need to make a decision on whether you want to purchase the tax lien or deed on a property or will you have to look up each property individually to find the information? Will you have access to maps or pictures of the property? Will you have access to prior lien information?

Register for the tax sales that you are interested in participating in as soon as registration is open for the auction. This will give you plenty of time to research the properties and to deposit money if a deposit is required. Don't do your due diligence on the tax sale properties too soon, though. If you do your due diligence a few weeks before the tax sale, chances are that at least half of the properties that you spent time researching will not be in the sale! Delinquent taxpayers have the opportunity to pay the taxes on properties and remove them from the tax sale up until the day that the sale begins, so pay attention to updates.

Make sure that you get your bid in before the sale ends. At some of these tax sales, properties are auctioned in batches and each batch ends at a certain time. Bids are not accepted after the deadline.

Use caution when bidding; make sure that you're bidding on the correct property. Once the winning bid is accepted, it cannot be withdrawn. You must pay for all of your successful bids by the deadline, or lose any of the liens or deeds that you won, and be barred from future tax sales. So make sure that you have the acceptable form of payment ready in time.

### When Are The Online Tax Lien Sales?

Now that you know what you need to do to invest in tax liens or tax deeds online, let's look at when these tax sales take place. Remember each county only has a tax sale once a year. Arizona counties have tax sales in February and March. Florida counties have their tax sales in May and early June. Maryland counties also have tax sales in May and June, and Colorado and Indiana tax sales are held in the fall. I think you'll find that many of the counties that have online tax sales make it easy for you to find the information that you need online.

### When Are The Online Deed Sales?

Each California County has a tax sale once a year, but they are staggered throughout the year. Florida counties have tax deed sales more often, usually at least once a month. Some of the larger Florida counties may have tax deed sales as often as once a week. The Michigan online tax sales start in late summer and finish in early fall. New York counties, like the California counties have tax sales once a year and are staggered throughout the year.

### Things to Watch Out For

It seems that when any county goes from having live tax sales to online tax sales there is a lot more bidding competition, sometimes making it not worth it to bid in those counties. What happened in the Douglas County Nebraska tax sale is an example….

Nebraska has an interest rate of 14% and the interest is not bid down at the tax sale. What is bid down is the percent ownership of the property should the investor foreclose. The lien is awarded to the investor willing to accept the lowest percent ownership in the property should the lien not redeem and the investor foreclose on the property. Because this leads to sticky situations where the investor only owns a piece of the pie so to speak, and there is no real incentive for the owner of the property to redeem the lien, many Nebraska counties use a random selection process instead of the bid down ownership method.

Before the Douglas County auction went online, all of their liens were awarded at 100% ownership, by random selection. When more than one investor bid on a property, the bid was awarded randomly. When Douglas county had its first online tax sale, some bids were awarded for as low as 1% ownership. The bidders who won these liens were institutional buyers, not new investors that didn't know any better. They bid 1% even in spite of a warning on the Douglas County tax sale web site not to bid less than 100%. Here is the warning that is posted on the auction website:

**"First Time Nebraska Tax Certificate Bidders – Mandatory Reading…."**

**"In all previous Douglas County tax certificate auctions, liens have been sold at one hundred percent ownership. Ownership of less than one hundred percent raises questions concerning title insurance and foreclosure rights. Be sure you know your rights before placing bids at less than one hundred percent ownership."**

Here is the strategy that these institutional bidders are using at these tax sales: They bid 100% on any properties that they think will not redeem, or that they have a chance of foreclosing on, but only 1% on the nice properties that they are pretty sure will redeem. Remember they are not bidding down the interest rate; if the lien redeems they will get 14% interest on their money. However, if it doesn't redeem and they foreclose they will only get a **1% interest ownership** in the property.

You may not want to play this game of bidding down the percent ownership of the property, but there are other online states to bid in that don't bid down percent ownership in the property. Instead, they either bid down the interest rate or bid up the price of the lien, which results in the same thing – effectively lowering your return.

In the states where the interest rate is bid down, it can be bid down extremely low. There is always a reason why the investors are willing to bid down that low. In Florida, there is a minimum 5% penalty. In Florida tax sales, the interest rate is frequently bid down to .25%. That is because bidders know that they will receive the 5% penalty instead of the .25% that they bid. For properties that redeem right away – a 5% return is excellent! In Arizona however, (Arizona is another bid down the interest state) there is no penalty, so the bidding is usually not bid down as low as it is in Florida.

If you're bent on getting those higher returns that you've been told you can get with tax liens, but you don't live in a lien state, or don't even live in the United States, there are a couple of alternatives. You can invest with a tax lien agent or a tax lien investing fund as we talked about in the previous chapter, or you could invest in secondary tax liens, which we'll talk about in the next chapter. First, let's discuss what foreigners need to do to invest in U.S. tax liens.

## Investing From Overseas

There are two things that foreigners need to have in order to participate in the online tax sales, or any tax lien sales in the U.S. for that matter. All bidders must have a U.S. bank account and a U.S. tax ID number. Years ago it wasn't so difficult to get an Individual Tax Identification Number (ITIN) from the IRS. Nevertheless, with everything that has happened since 9-11, it's quite a bit more complicated today. Now in order to get an ITIN number, you first have to have a U.S. business so that you can get an Employer Identification Number (EIN). Only then can you apply for an ITIN number.

The best way to do this is to set up a U.S. LLC, have the LLC apply for an EIN number and file a U.S. tax return (or show that you need to file a tax return), then you can apply for an ITIN number. Once you have a U.S. LLC and EIN number, your business will be able to open a U.S. bank account. I know it sounds complicated but once you have the EIN number, which should not take long to get, you can start investing in U.S. tax liens in the counties that allow foreign investors (not all counties allow foreign investors to participate unless they have a U.S. entity). When you actually receive profit from your liens, however, you will need to have an ITIN to complete a tax return.

There is one thing that I would like to caution you about. Many investors have heard of the double-digit returns possible with tax liens and they expect to get those high returns when they participate in the online sales. The online sales are heavily attended because anyone with a computer, a tax ID number, and a U.S. bank account, may bid at these tax sales. When new investors bid too high at these tax sales they don't get any liens. Do not expect to get double-digit returns at the online tax sales. Returns of 5% - 7% at these sales are more realistic. Double-digit returns are possible but not likely when investing at the online tax sales.

## Help For Foreign Investors

I have found a solution for foreign investors who want to invest in tax liens and tax deeds in the U.S. I found an attorney that will set up an LLC for you – in the state where you want to invest, and help facilitate getting your tax ID number and a US bank account. I have also found one state that will allow investors to register to bid at the tax sale without having to provide a tax identification number. They haven't quite figured it out yet, but once they do they will be requiring that information, but for now it's a good place for foreign investors to start while getting everything else in place.

# CHAPTER THIRTEEN: Secondary Tax Liens

### Are secondary tax liens for you?

There are two types of tax lien investors - those who invest to get high interest on their money and those who invest for the possibility of owning properties for the back taxes. Which are you? Tax liens are not a way to get property for back taxes, but it does happen occasionally. Investors who want to own property have a better chance of getting the property with redeemable deeds and tax deeds. However, there is another way to invest in tax liens and increase your chance of foreclosing on properties?

You can increase your chances of foreclosing on a tax lien by buying secondary tax liens from another investor that are ready to foreclose. Why would an investor want to sell you their lien when the redemption period is almost over? Some investors buy liens for the return they get and they are not interested in owning property. They may be investing from another state or from another country and don't want to go through the trouble of foreclosing and owning and managing the property. They would rather take their profit now than pay the foreclosure costs, wait for the lien to foreclose, and then have to deal with having to rehab, sell, or rent the property. They would much rather take a smaller return now then to have to go through the foreclose process, and put even more money out for the promise of a larger return later.

Large institutional tax lien buyers sell off their liens all the time, but they usually sell them in bulk to banks, fund companies, and large investors. They don't cater to small investors. Because they buy in such large quantities, they aren't always as careful with their due diligence as you would be when purchasing a tax lien with your own money.

One of the tax lien investing agents that I have recommended to my students for the last few years does sell secondary tax liens to individual investors. Because they purchase liens for individuals, not big fund companies, they are very careful with their due diligence. These liens are offered to members of the Tax Lien Profits Accelerator™ (Tax Lien Lady's Members Area).

## Chapter 13 Resources

**To get the replay of a webinar recording about how you can make money with secondary tax liens go to TaxLienInvestingSecrets.com/freebookbonuses**

# CHAPTER FOURTEEN: Investing For Your Future

## Profit Faster From Tax Liens with a Self-Directed IRA

I am not a financial planner or financial adviser - Far from it! I'm just an average person who really is not an expert in finances, real estate, or legal stuff. But I do know a few things about investing in tax liens. I have also learned a little bit about wealth building and money management. I've learned - sometime the hard way, about what not to do. And over the last few years, I've had the opportunity to meet people that are experts in wealth building and personal finance. In fact, I've interviewed quite a few experts and hosted some informative webinars for my subscribers. I have also invited them to speak at my tax lien investing conferences, so I'm always learning more about these things myself.

The reason why I'm so interested in personal finance and wealth building is that I had a little problem. Maybe you can identify with it as well, or maybe you're a little smarter and more disciplined with managing your money then I was. The problem is that I like to spend money. As a matter of fact, I can easily manage to spend all of the money I make, and maybe even a little more. Maybe you know someone, or a few people who have this problem too. It seems to be epidemic in our society. The good news is that I've learned to spend some of the money I make on investments - tax liens for the most part. In addition, my husband and I have learned to put a small portion of our income into a tax differed retirement account, so that when it comes time for us to retire, we have the income we need to maintain our standard of living. After all, at the rate our government is spending money, social security may not be there for some of us when we're ready to retire.

Back to my true confession about the way I used to handle the family finances, maybe it's something that you can relate to - I think that most Americans can. I like to spend money. After all, it's a lot more fun to spend money than it is to make it! So when a tax lien would redeem, instead of reinvesting that money, as I knew that I should, I had a tendency to use it to pay for things. Not extravagant things, but things like paying off unexpected bills, my kid's college tuition payments, or paying off debt.

I knew that I should be re-investing that money in more tax liens or using it to pay subsequent taxes on my existing liens. A few years ago a found a solution. I decided to start contributing to a self-directed IRA and invest in tax liens with money from my IRA. This way I would not really have control of the money. My IRA custodian would control it and I would not be able to spend the profit that came in from redeemed liens, it would go back into my self-directed IRA account to purchase additional investments. And, my profits would grow tax free until I took disbursements when I retired.

There are a few benefits to having a self-directed IRA. One of the benefits that I had immediately when I started contributing to my IRA is that the money that I contributed was deducted from my taxable income, which allowed me to get a bigger tax refund than I expected in some years and pay less taxes in other years. Other benefits to using a self-directed IRA to invest are that the money in your IRA is protected from creditors, and it can be handed down to your descendants without being taxed.

## Start Contributing to a Self-Directed IRA or 401(k)

If you have a 401(k) with your employer, that's good, but not as good as if you had a self-directed IRA or solo 401(k) that you can control. With a true self-directed retirement account, you have control and can invest in almost anything you want to, including real estate. I am not a retirement account expert, but I have interviewed a view retirement account specialists over the last few years. I've learned enough from them to prompt me to open SEP IRA accounts for myself and for my husband.

You have to have your own business to have a SEP IRA, and you cannot contribute to a SEP if you are contributing to a 401(k). A SEP IRA allows you to contribute a lot more per year than an individual IRA account does. I recommend that you talk to a representative from an IRA custodian about opening a true self-directed IRA that gives you control over your investments, so that you can open an account and start funding it. If you need help finding a self-directed IRA company, here are four that I have worked with that you can check out:

- IRA Services Trust
- Equity Trust Company
- CAMA Plan
- U Direct.

There are quite a few others but these are companies that I have done interviews, webinars or seminars with.

**What About A Roth IRA?**

Now that I'm getting closer to retirement age, a Roth IRA or Roth 401K account is looking more attractive. What is the difference between a Roth account and a regular IRA or 401K? With a Roth account, you contribute after tax money, so you pay the taxes on the money before you put it into your account. Just like a regular retirement account, you cannot take any money out of the account until you reach retirement age, but when you do take distributions – unlike with a regular account, the money is tax free! Therefore, not only can your profit grow tax free but it will be tax free for life.

# CHAPTER FIFTEEN: More Tips for Your Success

**Focus on Your Goals**

What are your goals for investing? It is important that you know what your goals are before you decide what and where to invest. If you're investing for immediate income, than tax liens would not be a good investment vehicle for you. Some investments are short term and some take longer to produce the desired result. Tax liens are a medium term investment. Depending on the state you invest in, you may not see your profit for anywhere from 1 to 3 years. Tax deeds and redeemable tax deeds are a shorter term investment but it still may be 6 months to 2 years before you can sell a property and collect your profit.

What kind of yield are you looking for and how much risk are you willing to take? Higher profit usually comes with a higher risk. What I love about tax lien investing is that you can get big profit without extremely high risk. Do you need to keep your investments liquid, which might be the case if you are retiring soon, or do you have some short terms goals that you need to meet?

Get clear on what your goal is for investing and then you can choose an investment vehicle that fits your goal. The first thing that I do with my members and coaching clients is find out what their goals are, how much money they have to invest, and where they live. Once I have that information, I can help them find the best place for them to invest, and the right vehicle to invest in, whether it is tax liens, redeemable deeds, tax deeds, secondary tax liens, or tax foreclosed properties.

**Map out Your Investment Strategy**

Once you know what your goal is and you have decided on your investment vehicle, then it is helpful to map out a strategy. What vehicle will you invest in? Where will you invest? How often will you need to add to your investment? How will you re-invest your profit?

With tax lien investing for example, you may want to pick one state to invest start in. Most states will have tax sales at only one time of the year, so you can plan how much money you will invest and what time of year you'll be investing. Then, depending on which state you invest in, you may also need to plan to pay the subsequent taxes. You will also know when the redemption period will end and when you're likely to get paid on your liens and can reinvest your profits.

**Reinvest Your Profits**

The first few years I invested in tax liens, when my tax liens redeemed, there was always something to spend the money on - bills, college tuition for one of my kids, or taxes to pay on real estate that I owned. However, I knew that for my money to grow, I had to re-invest my capital and profit. For some of us this is easy, but for others this may not be so easy. One way that I finally started doing this was to invest through a self-directed IRA instead of only investing after tax money. This insured that I re-invested my capital and any profit that I made.

I still do some investing outside of my self-directed IRA, but at least half of my investing is with money from my retirement account. That way I know that when these tax liens redeem all the money will be re-invested and I won't be tempted to spend it. So how do you know whether you should invest with IRA money or after tax money? That is a conversation you may want to have with your CPA, or financial advisor.

**Strategize With Your Accountant to Maximize Your Tax Situation**

Don't wait until tax time to sit down with your accountant or CPA. I usually like to talk to my accountant before the end of each year to see where I'll stand come tax time. There are things that you can still do even after the year is over to minimize your taxes or maximize your tax return - like contributing to your self-directed IRA. You can contribute to your retirement account through the date you file your tax return and have it apply to the previous year to lower your income and the amount of taxes you have to pay.

Some things however, have to be done before the end of the year. For instance if you know that you're going to owe a lot of taxes, you might want to pay outstanding bills and make tax deductible purchases before the end of the year rather than wait until the new year. On the other hand, if you know you are going to have a bigger tax debt next year than you have this year, you might want to wait and spend the money after the first of the year. Find a good accountant that can help you make the most of all the legal ways to minimize your tax dept.

**Protect Your Assets with a Trust**

For this step, you will need to talk to a good asset protection attorney who can help you set up the right kind of trust to protect your assets from a lawsuit or judgment. You never know what can happen in the future, and it's better to be protected than to be vulnerable to having everything that you have worked for all your life taken away from you.

You don't want to worry about your assets being tied up and not being readily accessible to your family if anything should happen to you. If you set up your trust correctly, your trust will live on when you die and your assets can be transferred to your beneficiaries without them having to pay inheritance tax on the assets that are held in the trust. There is a reason why the wealthy have trusts. I am not an expert in this at all; I recommend that you find an attorney that is. Look for an attorney who specializes in asset protection. One such attorney that I know is Tim Berry in Arizona. His company is The Tax Academy, LLC and his firm's website is www.TheTaxAcademy.com. You may want to find an asset protection attorney in your state.

# Conclusion & Resources

Tax lien investing is a great way to invest your money without the risk of the stock market, but as you have learned from Part I of this book, like any other high return investment there are some risks. Most of the risks can be mitigated by doing your due diligence and knowing what the rules are and what your rights and responsibilities are as a tax lien buyer. I hope that I've given you a good understanding of that in this book, but it would take an encyclopedia to give you all of the details for every state. Beware of the so-called experts who try to do this, because anyone that says they are an expert on tax lien investing everywhere in the country is not telling the truth. Even if they knew the laws of every state, the fact is that county treasurers and tax collectors can still dictate how the process is followed in their jurisdiction and it's not always cut and dry. Unless someone has actual experience investing in a particular state, or has contact with investors that do, they couldn't possibly know all of the details and nuances of how it's done. And not knowing the details can cost you money!

The best way to find out if this is something that you can do profitably on your own, is to get the results of past tax sales. Armed with this information and what you've learned in this book, attend tax sales in your area or the area that you want to invest in. If you would like some support, I have a membership web site with resources and monthly trainings available for you. You can get more information at www.TaxLienLady.com/Membership.htm.

Tax lien investing is not something that you do once and then forget about – this is not a park and prey method of investing. It's more of a hands on type of investment that you'll need to manage if you're doing it yourself. As with many other money making opportunities, most people find that they do better if they have a mentor or coach to keep them accountable and shorten their learning curve. If you would like to have someone hold your hand through your first tax lien or tax deed purchases, I have a coaching program where I do just that! It's called

Tax Lien Lady's Inner Circle Coaching. The first things that I do for you when you become a one of my students is to help you find the best place to invest based on how much money you have to invest, where you live, and where the best areas are for investing. You can find out more about the Inner Circle Coaching Program at www.TaxLienInvestingCoach.com.

As you learned in Part III of this book, there are passive ways to invest - with an agent or tax lien investing fund, if you don't have time to do the investing yourself. There are also shortcuts if you don't want to wait out long redemption periods. In Part II you learned about ways to streamline your investing and make it easier with automation. If you want more tips on tax lien investing, I have a wealth of information on all topics related to tax lien investing on my blog at www.TaxLienInvestingTips.com.

You can also get my free Tax Lien Tips Newsletter at www.TaxLienTipsNewsletter.com.

Wishing You Success and Encouraging You to Profit

Joanne

Tax Lien Investor, Author, Speaker, and Mentor
www.TaxLienLady.com

# Epilogue

## My Journey

This book has been all about helping you invest your money in highly profitable tax lien certificates and tax deeds. However, other things are just as important, if not more so, than financial success. "What good will it be for a man if he gains the whole world but forfeits his soul? Or what can a man give in exchange for his soul?" (Matt 16:26)

Sometimes we are so busy trying to make ends meet or trying to get ahead and be successful that we forget why we are doing it. All the money in the world did not help Steve Jobs when he died of cancer. Fortunately for Mr. Jobs, he enjoyed an accomplished life in which he contributed much to society and was able to enrich his own life and that of his family. But what about you, will you work hard to amass enough money to retire comfortably only to find out that you will not be around to enjoy it? What are you doing for your health? What about your spiritual welfare? If you believe in a creator and in life after death, where will you spend eternity? And if you do live a long life will you be healthy and fit, and be able to enjoy your latter years. For me, my health, wellbeing and connection with God and my fellow man are just as important, if not more so, than any financial success that I enjoy now.

I've been a fitness and nutrition buff for most of my life. I left my job working for a medical device company and became a personal fitness trainer in 1988. At that time, I was working on helping my company develop a balloon expandable stent – now widely used for coronary stenosis. I became a personal fitness trainer because I knew that with the knowledge I had about fitness and nutrition I could help people never need the surgery that my company's profits depended on. Quitting my job as a lab technician and going to work as a fitness consultant was a tough decision to make. I had just graduated with a bachelor's degree in Biochemistry from Rutgers University a couple of years before, after working my way through school part time, and now I was going in a totally different direction.

I have been an athlete my whole life. In my teenage years, I was a synchronized swimmer, in my early 20's I did some competitive barrel racing and I was a competitive bodybuilder. In my late 20's and early 30's I competed at power lifting and set some state drug free bench press records in New Jersey. Then when I was four months pregnant with my third child, I started Olympic-style weightlifting, something I always wanted to do. I entered my first local weightlifting competition a couple of months before my 35$^{th}$ birthday, and 2 months after delivering my third child, by C-section. It took me 4 years to get really good at it, but by the time I got to my early 40s I had become a master national and master world champion weightlifter.

I also started coaching weightlifting. I began coaching one of my sons when he was 10 years old, as well as some of the other boys who wanted to lift with him, including one of my nephews. Most of other boys weren't dedicated and disciplined enough to continue their training beyond a few weeks. My nephew was busy with other sports and wasn't dedicated to weightlifting, but he did get a good foundation and today he is 21 years old and has set some drug free powerlifting records in New Jersey. My son went on to become a national champion weightlifter and when he was only 18, he won the USA Weightlifting's American Open, Junior National Championship, and Collegiate Championship. Thanks to him and Peter Roselli, my coach and mentor since 1994, (and currently the high performance director for USA Weightlifting). I became the first women coach of a men's international weightlifting team in 2009, when I took my son and his teammates to the first youth world championships in Chang Mai, Thailand.

All during this time my husband and I had our ups and downs financially, you can read about my story and how I got started in tax lien investing in the book Trust Your Heart, Transform Your Ideas Into Income by Marnie Pehrson. This book contains the inspiring stories of 19 entrepreneurs who overcame the odds and created their own successful business from scratch. Things were going pretty good and my husband and I were on track to pursuing our financial success until a few things happened that changed the course of our finances and our life.

I'm not going to go into all that here, that is a topic for another book, but suffice it to say that sometimes in life, in order to get your attention, God has to hit you over the head with a two by four. That's what happened to my family over the last 4 years. My husband and I went through some unforeseen difficulties, including some personal and health problems with a couple of our kids. Then my husband had a shoulder injury on the job, and needed extensive surgery to repair a completely torn rotator cuff and bicep tendon on his right side. We had to hire an attorney to fight with his company to cover the surgery and give him worker's compensation.

Over a year later we finally got everything worked out for his surgery, but then he had some other health problems that delayed it even further. Almost 2 years after his injury, he finally did get the surgery he needed, but his company did not want to hold his job for him and they let him go. We were fortunate that he had a disability policy, which supplemented his worker's compensation, but our income from his job was still about half of what it had been when he was working. We also lost his benefits including health insurance. We now had to pay health insurance out of our own pocket. His shoulder is better than it was before the surgery, but it will never be as good as it was before the injury. He will always have limitations. He was a diesel technician and worked on commercial generators. He could no longer go back to the same work, or any mechanical work involving repetitive motion of his right arm. So now, in his early 50s, he has to find another line of work.

At the same time all this was happening, things were changing in my business. My husband's income had always paid the bills and the income from my business was just the icing on the cake – a little extra that allowed us to have another vehicle, travel occasionally, and go out to diner once in a while, help pay the tuition for our children's education and the taxes on our investment property. Now, all of the sudden, I had to rely on my business to provide more.

Just when I needed to invest more into my business, I now had to take more money from it just to make ends meet. All of my business is conducted online, and most of my income came from the sale of online courses, either programs or educational trainings that I had created or those from colleagues that I know and trust. When I started my business it was easy to market my tax lien investing programs and courses online. People actually received my e-mail messages, read them, and responded to them. But things have changed in the online business marketplace. Just getting the messages delivered has become tougher, and people are so inundated with marketing messages that it's more difficult just to get your messages read, let alone for people to take action and respond. The income from my business was not as dependable as it once was. Now I find that visitors to my website are not as interested in learning how to invest in tax liens as they are to having someone either take them by the hand and do it with them or do it for them. Hence I am re-inventing my business to offer done-with-you and done-for-you solutions to tax lien investing.

Two things got me through the last 4 years, my renewed faith in God and my tax lien investments. Really it was my faith that got me through, and my reliance on God to meet my every need, even when things look impossible, for "with God all things are possible." (Matt 19:26). When suddenly one of our sons was in trouble, it was my faith in God that sustained me. I turned back to the faith that I had when I was younger, before I had let it get "choked by life's worries, riches, and pleasures." (Luke 8:14, from the parable of the sower)

I was preoccupied with life's worries and riches, wanting to have the good life and be successful. Now there's nothing wrong with wanting to have a good life and financial success, the problem comes when you forget about everything else in order to get it. Some people forget about their health in pursuit of financial success, others forget about their family, and some of us forget about God, or at least we take those things for granted and don't give them a thought.

Although I had always spent some time (a minimal amount) in prayer or meditation, and considered myself a "spiritual" person, I hadn't been to any formal worship service in a couple of years. I sought out a Catholic church (the church that I had belonged to in my youth and felt comfortable in), and started attending mass. I actually started watching daily mass on television. After watching mass on Television for some time, I realized that I needed to worship with other believers, not just alone at home in front of the TV. I got in touch with a family friend who had moved into the area a couple of years ago and was attending a Catholic church. I started going to daily mass with her for a while, until I was ready to attend church on Sunday when there would be many people there. I became friends with a small group of people who attended daily mass in the morning. On Thursdays after the service, we would have breakfast together at a local diner. I met the pastor and went to confession, my first confession in over 30 years! I started receiving communion. I became part of this faith community and eventually so did my husband. I want to encourage you to seek out and become part of a faith community too, regardless of what faith you are. Find a group of like-minded people that you can not only spend time with, but also worship with and pray with. "For where two or three are gathered in my name, there am I with them." (Matt 18:20)

The tax lien investments that I had made years earlier and redeemed in these last couple of years have really been a blessing during this time. They've helped us to pay some unforeseen expenses and keep our heads above water. So whenever I have some extra cash, even if there are bills that are coming in and other things that I probably should be paying, I'll buy some small tax liens and invest in my future. I rely on Providence to meet my everyday needs, and he always comes through.

What are you doing that makes you feel good about yourself, lets you help others and is good for your health? If you can't think of anything now, you might want to start looking. Don't just work hard to get ahead and make money, leave a legacy by doing what you love and helping others and remember to do something for your health while you're at it!

Now, in my 50's, I don't always have the time to compete at weightlifting, but I still make the time to exercise and workout. I also enjoy coaching young kids. The point is that I have something that I enjoy doing that keeps me healthy, and allows me to contribute something of myself to benefit others. I love seeing the kids that I coach succeed at weightlifting, it gives them self-confidence and teaches them discipline and dedication.

Don't forget about your spirituality either. Some of us never stop to think about what is important and why we are here in the first place. What will become of your soul when you leave this world and go to the next? Have you spent any time thinking about why you are here, what your true purpose is in this life and what awaits you in the next? What a shame it would be to have all the wealth you want now and then leave it all behind with nothing to show for it. To have done nothing to lift your fellow man, or to have made this world a better place.

Wishing You Happiness and Well Being,

*Joanne Musa*

# Glossary

**Accelerated Tax Sale -** Tax lien sale in which a county/municipality is selling the current year's taxes, and not the previous year's taxes. There are no open taxes that can be paid on liens bought at an accelerated sale.

**Affidavit -** A sworn statement in writing. Whenever you have any recording, search, or foreclosure fees you need to give the tax collector an affidavit. You should also provide the tax collector with an affidavit for any subsequent taxes that you pay. This is the only way to ensure that you receive your subsequent tax payments with interest when the lien is redeemed. Some tax collectors also require affidavits to be notarized. Some states (such as Arizona) that keep all the records for you and do not issue a tax lien certificate to the investor do not require an affidavit. Some other states may have another form that the investor has to provide in lieu of an affidavit.

**Assignment -** Transfer of a tax lien certificate or tax deed from one individual or entity to another. For the transfer to be effective it must be registered with the county and filed with the tax collector. Usually there is a fee involved to record the assignment of a lien/deed. If the tax collector doesn't have record of the assignment, the taxing authority will pay the original owner of the tax lien certificate or tax deed when it is redeemed. In addition, if the assignment is not recorded then the property could be sold or foreclosed on and only the original lien holder will be notified, not the assignee.

**Bankruptcy -** There are different types of bankruptcy, however, each one is a legal action that either functions to protect the debtor from having to pay more money to creditors than he or she could possibly pay (in the case of a voluntary bankruptcy), or, in the case of involuntary bankruptcy, to insure that creditors are paid. When a person or entity files for bankruptcy, their property is turned over by the court to a trustee to insure payment to creditors. Once bankruptcy is filed, a federal judge will order a "stay" or freeze on any actions by creditors. Depending on what type of bankruptcy is filed, if you hold a lien on the property involved, you may have to file a claim with the bankruptcy court. In any case, you will be unable to foreclose on the property on which you have a lien until the stay is lifted.

**Bidder Information Sheet or Bidder Registration Form** - This is a form that you must fill out in order to bid at a tax sale. This form along with a W-9 form must be filled out and handed in either before you are allowed to bid or once you are a successful bidder, depending on the state and county you are bidding in. At some of the smaller live tax sales you will only be required to hand in these forms if you are the successful bidder on any liens. The Bidder Information form lists all your contact information, including your Social Security Number or federal ID Number (if you're bidding under a company name). There may also be a disclaimer on this form that you are required to sign in order to bid.

**Bring down** - Update to title search.

**Clean title** - Title to property that is free from any encumbrances. This type of title is usually not conveyed when you purchase property at a tax deed sale, nor when you foreclose on a tax lien property. Clean title to a property is conveyed with a warrantee deed, not a tax title deed, or quit claim deed. Most tax deed states deliver a tax deed or quit claim deed, not a warrantee deed. In order to clear the title on a tax foreclosed property it may be necessary to file a legal action known as a "quiet title action," or go through a "title certification process" with a title company.

**Face value** - The face value or face amount of a lien is the amount of the certificate along with any interest due, subsequent payments made by the certificate holder, interest due on the subs, and any fees incurred that will be refunded to the lien holder when the lien is redeemed. In other words, it is the amount that the lien holder would receive if the lien were to be redeemed. This value, of course, is dependent on the date of redemption.

**Foreclosure -** A legal procedure for a creditor to take possession of property in which the creditor has an interest, in order to receive payment of debt. Some states require legal action be taken to foreclose on a tax lien or tax deed and some do not. In some states the property owner can still redeem the property even after foreclosure. If you are foreclosing on a property in a state where court action is required, you should seek legal counsel. Foreclosure proceedings need to be followed according to the state laws or you could lose your rights to the property.

**Lien -** A legal claim against an individual's property for the satisfaction of a debt.

**Lien holder -** Person or entity in whose name a lien is registered in the county records against real property.

**Open Taxes -** Current unpaid taxes at the time of the tax sale. Most tax sales are for previous year's taxes, in which case there current taxes due that can be paid once you have the tax lien certificate, in states that allow you to pay them. This tax amount that can be paid after you own a lien is also referred to as **subsequent taxes** or **sub taxes** or simply **subs**.

**Over the counter liens or deeds -** Liens or deeds that were not sold at the tax sale and taken over by the county or municipality. In some states these liens and/or deeds are available for private bids. They are sometimes referred to as **left over liens or over the counter (OTC) liens or deeds**. "Over the counter" refers to the way they are purchased, by private bid and not at auction. If left over liens are available and purchased over the counter, they are usually available at the statutory interest rate. In some states, left over deeds can be purchased for less than the original minimum bid amount.

**Premium -** An amount paid to the county/municipality over and above the lien amount in order to win the lien (or deed) at auction.

**Prior lien holder -** A person or entity that holds a previous tax lien on a property.

**Realty Transfer Fee -** This is a fee that you may be required to pay in order to file a deed with the county clerk. In some states, any time real property changes hands it requires payment of a realty transfer fee.

**Recording or Filing Fee -** This fee is charged by the County Clerk for recording of the lien (or deed) with the county. A copy of the lien is filed in the county records. The tax lien certificate or tax deed is given a book and page number where it can be found in the county records. Most tax lien state allow this fee to be returned to the investor when the lien is redeemed (if an affidavit has been filed with the tax collector). Most states will require both liens and deeds to be recorded. There are a couple of states though that do not require the recording of liens, since all property transaction must go through the county treasurer. (Arizona in particular does not require the investor to record the tax liens, they do that for you and will charge you a processing fee.)

**Redeemable Deed -** Deed that is encumbered for a period of time during which it may be redeemed by the delinquent property owner. Usually there is a hefty penalty paid to the investor in order to redeem the deed.

**Redemption:** A tax lien certificate is redeemed (the lien is satisfied) when the owner pays the tax collector the amount of the lien plus any subsequent payments, interest, and penalties. In most states the redemption is paid to the tax collector. The investor must send the tax lien certificate in to the tax collector to collect payment.

**Redemption Penalty -** A redemption penalty is assessed to the property owner upon redemption of the lien or redeemable deed. A penalty differs from an interest rate in that it is not calculated per annum. Some tax lien states also have a penalty in addition to the interest accrued. Some states (Florida for instance) will pay a penalty amount rather than an interest rate.

**Redemption Period -** The time frame that the delinquent tax payer has to redeem a tax lien or redeemable deed. If a lien is not redeemed within the redemption period, the purchaser of the lien can either foreclose on the property or apply for a deed, depending on the state. If a redeemable deed is not redeemed within the redemption period, the tax lien purchaser can obtain the property either through a judicial foreclosure or deed application process. Redemption periods vary greatly among states, and can be anywhere from 6 months to 3 years depending on the state.

**Sewer Lien (most frequent type of utility lien) -** This is a lien placed on a property for sewer taxes. Sometimes there are more sewer liens available than tax liens due to the fact that in many cases the mortgage company pays the property taxes, but the homeowner pays the sewer taxes. In some states unpaid sewer amounts (as well as water bills, maintenance fees, and other utility amounts) can be sold at the tax sale. A tax lien certificate issued for these amounts carries the same weight and privileges for the lien holder as does a tax lien.

**Special Assessments -** These are assessments levied by the city or municipality for various reasons. They are not extinguished by a tax sale and must be paid by the purchaser of a tax deed. They also need to be paid by the purchaser of a tax lien in order to foreclose if the lien is not redeemed. In some states, these amounts can also be sold in the tax sale and a tax lien certificate is issued just as for sewer or water liens, or other utility liens.

**Subsequent Taxes -** Also referred to by investors as "**subs**." In many states, once you own a tax lien certificate, you can pay any subsequent taxes when the owner is delinquent in paying them. The timing in which you can pay the subsequent taxes depends on the state. Some states collect taxes annually and others collect taxes more often. In

New Jersey, taxes are paid quarterly and are considered delinquent on the 10th of the month in which they are due.

In Florida, you do not pay the subsequent taxes on a tax lien, instead another lien will be sold the following year if the taxes are not paid by the property owner. When the redemption period is over and it's time to apply for the lien to be sold in a deed sale, then all the subsequent taxes are paid and subsequent liens redeemed. The investor gets the statutory interest (18%) on all the sub tax payments from here on. In states that do allow you to pay the subsequent taxes, it's a good idea to pay the subs as soon as you can. This is because in most states you earn the statutory interest on the subsequent tax payments and it will keep the property from being sold in next year's tax sale.

**Tax Deed -** Some states do not sell tax liens. If you are delinquent in paying your property taxes, they sell the deed to your property. Some states that sell tax deeds provide a redemption period in which the owner can redeem his or her property even after it is sold in a tax sale and some do not.

**Tax Lien -** A legal claim on someone's property for the satisfaction of a debt related to taxes.

**Tax Lien Certificate -** This is a certificate of sale for unpaid municipal or county liens, issued by the tax collector of a municipality or county tax collector or treasurer, verifying payment. The certificate lists the certificate number, name of the tax collector, the taxing district, the date of the sale. Also on the face of the certificate is the buyer's name and address, a description of the property (in New Jersey, block, lot and address of the property is listed. In most other states it's a parcel number and address of the property that is listed on the certificate), the name of the property owner, and the amount of the sale. The certificate is not valid unless it is signed by the tax collector and notarized. Keep your tax lien certificates in a safe place. You must sign the back of the certificate, usually in front of a notary, and return it to the tax collector before receiving payment upon redemption by the property owner. Not all states will issue a tax lien certificate and in states that do, sometimes it is referred to by a different name, like **tax title** or **tax bill**.

**Quiet title** – This is a legal action taken to quiet the title to a property that does not have clear title. When the quiet title action is completed, title to the property is cleared and a warranty deed can be issued. You need clear title in order to get title insurance on a property, which mortgage lenders will require.

**Utility lien** - Lien on a property for unpaid utilities - can be unpaid sewer, water, or electricity or other service that is billed by a local government agent.

**W-9 form** – This is a tax form that you give to the tax collector if you are successful bidding at a tax lien sale or in the case of online tax sale, that you fill out online. The form lists your name or your company name and your tax ID. This information may also on the Bidder Information Sheet, or Bidder Registration Form, but at live tax sales, you may be required to submit both forms.

**Warranty deed** - Deed to a property that conveys clear title to a property.

**Year End Penalty** - This is an extra penalty added onto tax liens in some New Jersey municipalities only. It only applies to subsequent tax payments in excess of $10,000.00. If the amount of subsequent taxes paid by the lien holder is $10,000.00 or more at the end of the tax year, an extra 6% penalty is added (payable to the lien holder upon redemption of the lien) on January $1^{st}$ of the following year. This is not statewide; it is up to the tax collector to decide whether they have this penalty or not.

# About The Author

**Joanne Musa,** the Tax Lien Lady, known online as America's most trusted teacher and trainer on tax lien investing, helps investors who want to reap the rewards of from safe, profitable tax lien certificates and tax deeds. For more than 10 years, Joanne has specialized in training people on how to build a profitable portfolio of tax lien certificates or tax deeds, so that they no longer need to take their chances in the stock market.

Joanne is a contributing author to the book "The Venus Approach To Real Estate Investing" and the Amazon Best Seller "Trust Your Heart: Transform Your Ideas Into Income." She has been featured in the online Publications NuWire Investor and Foreclosure News Report. She has also been featured on the real estate investing web sites REIWired.com, Foreclosure.com, and REIBlueprints.com, and has been interviewed by Forbes Magazine.

Joanne has taught thousands of people from all over the world how to get double-digit returns on their money without the risk of the stock market. She has interviewed top experts from around the country on all aspects of tax lien and tax deed investing to bring her subscribers and customers the best and most current information available. Her articles on tax lien and tax deed investing appear all over the Internet. Her easy to follow step-by-step guides and no-nonsense approach and to investing in tax lien certificates and tax deeds have earned her the reputation of being the most trusted tax lien investing authority online.

Joanne lives in East Stroudsburg in the Pocono Mountains of Pennsylvania with her husband and three sons. Before becoming a tax lien investing trainer and educator, she was a personal fitness trainer for more than 10 years. She is also a Master National Weightlifting Champion and Master World Champion Weightlifter. She still trains and is a USA Weightlifting coach. In 2009 she became the first women coach of an international men's weightlifting team when she took her son and 7 other young men to lift in the first Youth World Weightlifting Championship. Joanne also holds a Bachelor of Arts degree in Biochemistry from Rutgers University.

## How to Contact Joanne

The best way to ask me a question is to fill in the Ask The Tax Lien Lady form on my blog at TaxLienInvestingTips.com - you'll also find a lot of articles and free information there about investing in tax liens and tax deeds.

You can also find me on Facebook at Facebook.com/TaxLienInvestingTips

on LinkedIn at Linkedin.com/in/joannemusa

on my YouTube Channel at YouTube.com/taxlienlady

And you can always reach me through my customer support manager at support@taxlienlady.com.

*Exclusive Free Bonuses For Readers Only...*

# Get Your Free Bonuses For Reading This Book!

As a special thank you gift for reading this book I invite you to claim your FREE bonuses!! Register to claim your free bonuses at the website below, including the webinar replays that are mentioned in the resource section of Chapter 11 and Chapter 13. However, that's not all you'll get when you claim your free bonuses for reading this book. You will also be able to download valuable resources from a couple of the most trusted real estate investing trainers in the US, and Tax Lien Lady's State Guide, which gives a summary of how tax sales work in each state and lets you know which states sell tax liens and which sell tax deeds. Plus, you'll get my Sweet 16 Tax Sale Websites swipe file – links to 16 little known tax sale websites that you can access for free. And you'll get discounts to services that will help you with your tax lien and/or tax deed investing. Take advantage of these valuable bonuses now at:

www.TaxLienInvestingSecrets.com/freebookbonuses